CONFIDENTLY LOST

CONFIDENTLY LOST

'Heartfelt, honest and hugely comforting.'
DONNA ASHWORTH

Finding **joy** in the chaos and rediscovering what matters most in life

GAVIN OATTES

CAPSTONE
A Wiley Brand

Registered Offices
John Wiley & Sons, Inc., 111 River Street, Hoboken, NJ 07030, USA
John Wiley & Sons Ltd, New Era House, 8 Oldlands Way, Bognor Regis, West Sussex, PO22 9NQ, UK

For details of our global editorial offices, customer services, and more information about Wiley products visit us at www.wiley.com.

The manufacturer's authorised representative according to the EU General Product Safety Regulation is Wiley-VCH GmbH, Boschstr. 12, 69469 Weinheim, Germany, e-mail: Product_Safety@wiley.com.

Library of Congress Cataloging-in-Publication Data is Available:

ISBN 9780857089984 (Paperback)
ISBN 9780857089991 (ePub)
ISBN 9781907312533 (ePDF)

Cover Design and Image: Peter Cotter

Set in 10/14pts and Adobe Caslon Pro by Straive, Chennai, India.

Printed and bound in Great Britain by Bell & Bain Ltd, Glasgow

For...

The silly hearts.

Anyone who's ever felt like too much and not enough, all at once. Those of us wandering the dinner hall of life, tray in hand, wondering where to sit. And those who carry glitter in their bones and thunder in their chest.

I hope you win the war you tell no one about.

Contents

Foreword

I love words but I was wordless, which was making it tough to write a foreword! And then I found one, *ineffable*. Ineffable means 'unspeakably beautiful and moving'.

In the liminal space of Gavin's suffering, that space between the no longer and the not yet, he wrote this book . . . Isn't that just, well, *ineffable*.

Gavin is a natural at being himself. There are a small, distinct group of people in my life that I feel 'me' with, and Gavin is one of them. In the time I spend with him I get back in my bones. The thing is you didn't know you had left your bones until you spend time with him.

Whether you are watching him on stage, reading his books or eating kippers with him in a randomly chosen café, he shows you where the life is in the moment. He gets you to be here, he gets you to remember. You can watch him soak up the whole world, he is *constantly* paying attention which is unbelievably generous because that hurts.

He encourages you to extend yourself some grace *and* skip to the toilet. He is a walking paradox. I can be with Gavin and laugh until wee comes out *and* then fling myself back in my seat and exhale, *ooft*, when he delivers a one-liner packed with flair . . . and some fucks.

Gavin has this uncanny ability to be both teacher and friend, to make you laugh while holding up a mirror that finally allows you to see yourself clearly. In a world where we're constantly told who to be, how to be, when to be, he gives you permission to simply be.

Remember that kid in school who you stared at when they put up their hand and they said, 'eh Sir, I don't get it'. And then you felt your whole body decompress where even your cells felt relieved as you appreciated, you aren't the only one. That's like sitting with Gavin.

He 100% gives a shit.

When I first read this book, I cried. How irresponsible of me, get some tissues.

Now. Stop, put the book/iPad/tablet down, pause the audiobook and just find the tissues.

This will tinker with your emotions. The exquisite nature of Gavin's writing is that you will laugh and cry until you cry again. The tears come from different places (not physically, that's a terrible visual). Places of recognition, relief, joy, delight, the tender ache of truth.

It is a full-body experience.

This is a bringer of joy, a contemplation of you-ness, a comedy sketch and a best friend all wrapped into *304 pages.*

In these pages, what he has managed to do, with grace, elegance and a smidgen of swearing, is help us understand what holds us together. I don't mean the atoms and quarks and muscly bits. I mean where do we go, who do we speak to, who do we avoid (you know, the ones that deserve a wedgie), what glimmers do we seek, to feel held together?

To feel like you've got this. To feel like you. That delightfully unique you-ness that life tries hard to make you forget. He got me thinking again, what is a Kirsty, what is it like to be me? And I had forgotten.

When you were younger were you ever told you were 'full of yourself'? Those words were not necessarily said in the most encouraging of tones, but, at the tender age of 50, I want to be FULL of myself again. A lot of us have full schedules, full minds, full washing baskets but not a full heart.

Often we feel dragged through life and we make ourselves busy, unavailable, distant, too available . . . and sick. I wonder what part of us is a coping mechanism for the world and what is actually, us? Sometimes we let others decide who we are.

The invitation here is that, maybe, this life we are all living *is* rigged for our growth and joy after all. Gavin gets you to trust in the disorientation and chaos that is happening, and is *going* to happen, and yet, reassures your nervous system that it's ok to be here. And maybe we shall find out we don't need the word resilience as much if we were just kinder to one another.

This looks like a book, smells like a book (or a Kindle) but is so much more.

Wow, ok Kirsty, chill. Next you are going to tell us he will give you the answer to world peace. Well, he does. And it involves cakes. And your Granny.

Does this book give you the meaning of life? No, but maybe it offers you the meaning of you.

As Rick Rubin says, it rings true. It harkens back to some truth in the universe.

You deserve these words; these glimmers, multiple sunkicks, and the world deserves you.

With a glass of diluting juice, let your busy mind sit in the corner as you read this. May you feel it in your bones. And today, maybe, skip (to) class.

Gav, thanks.

Whilst you say you wrote this for you, my God, you wrote this for us too. You have shown me that suffering is an act of solidarity, that tenderness is an act of freedom, that skipping is the best way to travel and that my boyfriend was born on Penis Island.

You are a sunkick personified.

Written by Kirsty Joy Grace HOPE Mac

Kirsty Mac is a renowned coach, speaker and writer.

CHAPTER 0.5

21st Century Breakdown

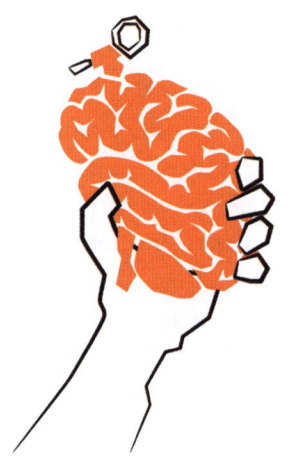

L

et's begin with a quote . . .

'I think there is pressure on people to turn every negative into a positive, but we should be allowed to say, 'I went through something really strange and awful, and it has altered me forever'.

Marian Keyes

Think of this peculiar 'chapter' as a scene setter, providing essential context. It's not really a chapter, nor is it technically part of the book, yet it serves as the catalyst for the next 62,000 words. A moment, born out of a pivotal experience, that has changed everything for me. Forever.

My writing journey for this book reminds me of Green Day and their journey to creating 'American Idiot'. They had an entire album ready to go, but when those recordings were stolen, they didn't give up. Instead, they poured their hearts and souls into creating something entirely new, a masterpiece.

I was well under way with my new book. It had a clear focus and felt more business-like. Personally, I was in a good place, very fit, having lost a lot of weight and feeling incredibly healthy. I distinctly remember a conversation with my wife where I told her, 'I don't think I've ever been happier'.

And then everything changed.

'All great changes are proceeded by chaos'.

Anon

The days, weeks and months that followed? A total blur. But one thing is clear, out of nowhere and completely beyond my control, my past came crashing into my present, shattering my reality in the most messed-up way imaginable. The result? Anxiety dialled up to eleven, a year in therapy and my first uneasy introduction to antidepressants.

I was lost.

This is *not* a book about what happened, but rather a book inspired by events in which my world shifted, and how, as humans, we navigate the aftermath of profound disruption, discovering resilience, growth and new beginnings.

What emerged from that upheaval is the heart of this book.

Lifequake

Noun / lahyf-kweyk /

A significant, sudden an unexpected shift in the trajectory of your life that initially feels devastating but has the beneficial outcome of catalysing personal growth, transformation and rebirth.

My 'American Idiot' moment. A moment when my 'best year ever' took an unexpected turn, leading to something I never could have anticipated. But in my story, it wasn't my work that was stolen from me, it was so much more. I was robbed of my peace of mind, my time, my focus, my sense of security, my sleep and my joy.

I was robbed of everything that matters.

This is not the book I planned to write, but it's the one that came out. It's the book I was *meant* to write, and I warn you now, if you choose to keep reading, I might just brainwash you into believing in yourself and rediscovering what you're capable of!

I chose not to give up, I found my way, I rediscovered joy and you can too. Oh, and whilst I would never claim this to be my masterpiece, in the words of Green Day . . .

'For what it's worth, it was worth all the time'.

CHAPTER 1

It's Hard to Be a Person

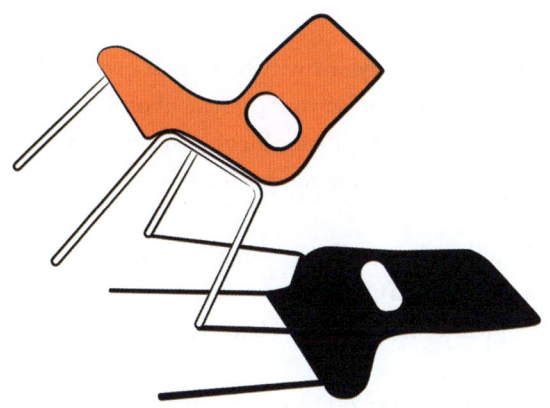

t's me.

Hi.

I'm the problem.

It's me.

Yes, I just opened with a Taylor Swift lyric. Don't worry though, whether you're a Swiftie or not won't affect your enjoyment of this book. It's not about the song or even knowing who Taylor Swift is. It's the words. Words matter, and these words perfectly capture the essence of what I'm about to share.

My daughter introduced me to Taylor's music, starting with 'Anti-Hero'. For the record (pun unintended), I absolutely love it. Regardless of genre or artist, a great tune is a great tune, and 'Anti-Hero' is *such* a tune!

I couldn't name many of her other songs, but when I heard the chorus of 'Anti-Hero', it was a lightbulb moment. Actually, it was more than that, it was like the entire lightbulb aisle at the hardware store suddenly illuminating.

After years of self-doubt, people-pleasing, seeking validation and battling fear and anxiety, I had a moment.

An 'I'm Taylor Swift' moment?

Not quite . . .

It was more of a 'Fuck, it's me. I'm the problem' realisation.

'We may think of ourselves as static anti-heroes, but in reality we're just waiting for our courage to kick in'.

Justin Alcala

My very next thought was, 'Does this make *me* an anti-hero?' which was then *very* quickly followed by 'What's an anti-hero?', I genuinely had no idea, I'd never actually had to think about it before!

After many, *many* listens, I think Taylor is telling us that she – the anti-hero in her story – is ultimately a nice person with good intentions, but that she has a load of flaws and can, at times, be very, very self-destructive.

Well, if this is the definition of an anti-hero . . .

It's me.

Hi.

I'm the problem.

It's me.

Surely I'm *not* the problem though when kindness is *always* front and centre with me, the fact I want nothing but good in the world, I work hard, I'm incredibly loving, giving, hugely respectful and I genuinely just want everyone to be happy?

But that right there is the plot twist, even with all those positive qualities, we can still be our own greatest obstacle.

Ultimately, it boils down to this, like actual Taylor Swift, and many other humans, I'm not always good for me.

And that's the problem . . . the problem is me.

This realisation opens up a world of questions: Can we become our own anti-heroes? What does that mean for our personal growth? Are we all walking that fine line between hero and anti-hero in our own stories?

I invite you to reflect on these questions throughout this book.

Are you, perhaps, the Wolverine of your own narrative? Do you have a touch of Maleficent's complexity? Is there an Arya Stark within you, defying expectations?

Trust me, I know I'm already *definitely* overthinking this!

'To be nobody but yourself in a world which is doing its best day and night to make you like everybody else means to fight the hardest battle which any human being can fight and never stop fighting'.

EE Cummings

Research tells us that all anti-heroes are, deep down, good people. Authentic, independent and courageous, we're told they can offer a refreshing perspective on life. We're told they reject traditional societal expectations and forge their own path. We're told anti-heroes are creative, innovative and unafraid of self-discovery. And we're told they're good at embracing the complexities of their character, even the darker impulses.

Nice, this all feels familiar to me and I'm confident enough to claim I'm ticking *all* the boxes, what could possibly go wrong?

Well, we're also taught that anti-heroes often feel isolated. Unfulfilled, lonely and insecure, we're told they often find themselves in cycles of negativity and stagnation. We're told anti-heroes often have a face that doesn't fit with societal norms and often struggle to accept that this is ok. We're told anti-heroes are often racked with feelings of guilt, regret, often undermining their own feelings of happiness and contentment.

Dear reader, the anti-hero isn't some distant, fictional character. The anti-hero might just be the person staring back at you in the mirror; complex, flawed and beautifully human.

And we're told that over time they experience the consequences of these things, many of which can be detrimental to wellbeing.

Fuck.

It's me.

Hi.

I'm the problem.

It's me.

'I feel so alone – no one could ever understand this feeling' thought a thousand people, together, in unison.

Parm K.C.

This Is How It Feels to Be Me

Imagine you were back in school, about 10 years old and you're swinging on your chair. I'm sure we've all done it. Much of the time I didn't even realise I was doing it. As I sit here reminiscing, I'm actually quite proud of my ability to hit that sweet spot of balance at such a young age. That awesome song (Defying Gravity) from Wicked could have been written for me. Holy shit, maybe I'm Elphaba! Elphaba Swift . . .

Of course, it was against the school rules to swing on your chair. It was all about being able to hold it long enough, teetering on the edge of being a rule breaker or a class conformer. And if you didn't get caught or fall then it was a fleeting triumph in the art of young rebellion.

But swinging on your chair in class isn't all fun and games, is it? It's not all sweet spots and defying gravity (Honestly, such a tune. And film!). I'm not even talking about when you fell and hit the ground, sure that wasn't fun and the teacher was furious, but we all know, don't we, there is only one thing more terrifying than actually falling, and that's 'nearly falling'. Falling sucked, but *nearly* falling? Awful. That horrific moment is unrivalled in life's 'shit yourself' moments!

It didn't last long but it was enough to make you shit yourself good and proper. Not even half a second and your life momentarily unravelled, flashing before your eyes. A lightning bolt of top-rate panic ripping through your entire being. Head to toe.

I have been on some of the world's biggest rollercoasters and yet nothing even comes close to the fear generated by a 'nearly fall'. A teeter to the extreme.

But when you saved it . . . wow!

There is no better feeling than a 'nearly fall' saved. If you were to film someone swinging on their chair, nearly falling, but then saving it, and watch it back in slow motion, it would be like nothing you've ever seen. A ballet of emotions, arms and legs moving in ways not even invented yet. Science wouldn't be able to explain it. Facial expressions we can't even comprehend.

Gravity well and truly defied! And with that moment comes utter relief.

Even with the magnificent relief that follows, as good as that feels, a 'nearly fall' leaves you well and truly shot to shit! That half second of near death takes a good few minutes to recover from.

Now, imagine this . . .

You're swinging on your chair, you swing too far and just before you save it, there it is, as always, your half second of impending catastrophe. Ooft, every nerve in your body screaming with unease. Your heart and lungs leading the way to absolute physical and mental distress.

And then . . . as if by magic, someone presses pause.

On you.

Right in that horrible moment.

Pause.

For four months.

Four.

This too shall pass

(but holy fuck)

You see, anxiety for some of us isn't a little bit of sweating and a racing heart. It's *not* worrying. Adding to the already physical and mental distress, it's a lack of appetite, zero sleep, the inability to sit still, to focus, it's body pain, it's intense loneliness, it's thundering doubts and overwhelming sadness. It's teetering, in darkness, and it's debilitating. It's crippling.

'I don't have anxiety, I have "What-if?" Olympics'.

Anon

Experts often conceptualise anxiety with words/phrases such as 'a multifaceted construct, encompassing emotional, cognitive, and physiological dimensions, with dysregulation in one domain amplifying the impact across the entire spectrum of human experience'.

That last part though; **'amplifying the impact across the entire spectrum of human experience'.**

This. *Exactly* this!

Now let me put in my own words . . .

It fucks me up. And because of this, it affects every ounce of my life; the entire spectrum. That includes the lives of others, those around me, my family and my colleagues. It makes my job damn hard, and I hate what it does to me.

It's quite literally the opposite to hitting the sweet spot of balance in life. My inner ninja, with his remarkable ability to bend without breaking, the very same one that saved me so many times in my formative years from falling, now – in his 40s – has failed me.

Again.

Again?

This is the third huge run-in I've had in the last six years. I've written and spoken many times about my anxiety, it's something I've lived with forever. But this? This was the worst yet, next level. I couldn't leave my house, never been so scared and I've never cried so much in my life.

'Overheard a child at the park today tell his sad friend "It's ok to be sad. Sad stands for Secretly A Dinosaur". Then he let out a big roar'. "That kid is going places."

Matthew Pepper

Some people see anxiety as a weakness, I hope these same people never have to understand the strength it takes to come through it. At my lowest moments, I couldn't see a way back. I questioned how much more I could take. In my darkest moments, I wasn't sure I wanted to fight this fight.

Mental health challenges aren't always at 3 a.m., sometimes it hits you at 3 p.m. in the middle of a meeting. Sometimes it hits at 9 p.m. when you're with your friends and you're halfway through a hilarious conversation, pissing yourself laughing and suddenly you just stop.

Have you ever been so anxious in public that your brain, in all its survival wisdom, suggests, *Do a fake faint. Right here. Dramatically. Shut your eyes and take the floor.'* I have. Many times. Full-on, Oscar-worthy floor flops feel like the only escape route. I've never actually done it, but in the moment, the sheer absurdity of it almost calms me. Almost.

Anxiety is always feeling like there is something out of place, something wrong. And when you can't find what it is, unfortunately, you start to believe it's you.

'Having anxiety is the most painful experience. It makes no sense, and you sit there alone and suffer for an unknown reason'.

Anon

I had that feeling when you don't even know what the fuck you're feeling. I had to dig deeper than I ever thought possible. Everything I'd learned in the past failed me. All my tools and tricks, nothing was working. I watched everything I could online, read a multitude of books and blogs, re-read all my favourites. Everything I tried seemed utterly ineffective. The 'what if's?' and the 'why me's?' just kept coming, snowballing, getting bigger and bigger.

I did all the things, the journaling, the meditating, the spirit-lifting sprinkles allegedly sourced from Himalayan goat breath (not really). And still, I was knee-deep in lavender-scented anxiety (really).

Unpopular opinion: the wellness industry is not well. Wellness might be the word on everyone's lips, but are we all feeling well? If this is what 'well' looks like, maybe we need to redefine it, because behind the green juices and gratitude journals, there's exhaustion, anxiety and a whole lot of pretending. And pretending isn't healing. It's hiding. All the turmeric in the world won't fix what we're too scared to talk about.

I began to wonder if it might be easier for everyone if I wasn't here.

And then one day, in our back garden, a glimmer . . .

A Glow in the Dark

In its simplest form, a glimmer is a lovely wee something that makes you smile, an unexpected moment that gives you a lift, a little victory that can make your day. A hot bath, the sound of the birds, a massive crisp, a cup of tea, a particular song, a hug, even the sound of the ice cream van.

But, glimmers are *so* much more than that, and to do them justice, they deserve a proper grand introduction, after all, this entire book has kinda been inspired by them, so here goes.

Deep breath . . .

At their best, glimmers are the unexpected bursts of magic that catch us off guard, lifting us from the depths and guiding us towards brilliance. They're the sparks that ignite within us, illuminating paths we never knew existed. In moments of uncertainty, they're tiny beacons of hope, shining through the darkness with a promise of possibility.

Glimmers fuel our creativity, setting ablaze our imaginations with the light of new beginnings. Sometimes fleeting moments, sometimes lifelines, offering joy, comfort, hope and the courage to persevere, glimmers are essential for maintaining resilience and mental wellbeing.

But there's more. Beyond their individual impact, glimmers are the threads that weave us together as a community, inspiring kindness, belongingness, compassion and collective action. In their radiance, we find unity and the power to transform the world.

A bold statement, I know!

'*Plunge deep enough in order to see something that is hidden and glimmering*'.

Matsuo Basho

But while we go huge with talk of changing the world – based on what you've just read – it may seem strange that we are not talking about great big, life-changing moments. A reminder: glimmers are micro-moments of goodness, they're freshly baked bread, a small act of kindness, a cosy blanket, a smile, a thank you, dogs, cats, or even the single guitar chord that rings out from a dimly lit stage.

A glimmer is a wonderful, calming, uplifting, occasionally inspiring, kick up the ass. It's the moment the sun catches your face. It's a sunkick, a sunkick up the ass!

Taylor Swift sunkicked my ass!

Kicking the Habit

Let me introduce you to the idea of Sunkicks. First, I'll define a sunkick in the style of an actual dictionary.

Sunkick (noun)

1. A brief, yet profound, surge of euphoria and elation experienced in life's ordinary moments, reminiscent of a sunbeam breaking through the clouds on a gloomy day. An instant of pure delight that uplifts the spirit and fills the heart with warmth and contentment.

Example: 'As she watched her child's laughter dance in the afternoon sunlight, she couldn't help but feel a sunkick wash over her, a fleeting but profound moment of joy that illuminated her soul with radiant happiness'.

Not sure I have a future in writing dictionary entries but in its essence, a sunkick transcends the mundane, reminding us of the inherent beauty found in life's simplest pleasures.

I often describe a sunkick as not being the same thing as a glimmer. A sunkick is more a mindset, it's not just a moment. In the example above, the child's laughter is the glimmer, the result is the sunkick, it's the illumination of her soul. Like any other mindset, it's a choice, you need to be present in order to notice the glimmer, but then choose to let it work its magic.

So, the glimmer is the thing and the sunkick is the outcome? Yes, but you need to embrace the thing fully in order to experience the outcome.

You still with me?

To me, a sunkick mindset asserts that within every individual lies the potential to draw energy and inspiration from the radiant positivity of life experiences. This is about turning the everyday grind into your own personal playground. I like to think of it as the middle finger to mediocrity. Just as the sun infuses the world with warmth and light, so too can we harness the metaphorical rays from our glimmers.

But how do we start, Gavin? How do we get our glimmer on?

We'll get there, I promise!

Weird Science

I ain't no scientist, but a glimmer is essentially the opposite of a trigger. Whether it's the sound of a siren, seeing an old photo or smelling a particular food, our minds can quickly associate these cues with either negative or positive emotions. Triggers are cues that signal to our brain that we are in danger, whereas glimmers are cues that signal safety, granting us permission to let go.

According to Dr Stephen Porges' Polyvagal Theory, the nervous system plays a pivotal role in shaping our individual emotional and behavioural responses to our surroundings. Central to this regulation is something known as the Vagus Nerve, which modulates our heart rate.

Just as the body combats illness, the nervous system possesses the capability to ward off negative emotions by activating the Ventral Vagus. A glimmer is effectively a brief moment of engagement with the Ventral Vagus, highlighting the body's innate capacity for emotional regulation.

As humans we are incredible. Without even knowing it, we're like the conductor of our own emotional orchestra, conducting an entire symphony of feelings!

According to *The Polyvagal Theory in Therapy: Engaging the Rhythm of Regulation* by Deb Dana, in our overstimulated world, these lovely, warming, contented moments are not just pleasant and comforting, but they may actually be the answer to regulating our overwhelmed nervous systems. Get it right and we're no longer in the school band, we're in the goddamn London Symphony Orchestra!

Whelmageddon

As for an overwhelmed nervous system, my overwhelm was so overwhelming that my overwhelm was overwhelmed.

I'm not entirely sure what the recommended dose of whelm is these days, but I'm pretty certain I was scaling new heights and setting records. Maybe someone knows the answer but is any amount of whelm actually good for us?

I believe 'as fuck' to be a fabulous unit of measurement, and I am very comfortable sharing that I was whelmed as fuck!

On the outside I may appear to some as fairly nonchalant, but on the inside, I am forever utterly chalant, never *not* chalanting, like a pro! Someone once told me my biggest weakness is that I care too much.

But, I was triggered and I needed to find out how to *un*trigger myself. There's no quick fix in these situations, I knew it was going to take time and effort. There was so much going on in my head. Huge strength was needed to work through it and find my way again.

Some of you will know what I mean when I say I was dreaming of the moment I finally stop thinking about how I was feeling.

For very different reasons I'd been here before, so knew that I needed to find my 'package' of support that would lift me. It's never just one thing though, and finding the correct formula is exhausting.

My research tells me that the journey of an anti-hero is never just a straight line, it's a wild, unpredictable ride filled with twists, turns and moments of self-discovery.

But there was no journey, currently. Twists and turns definitely, accompanied by familiar feelings of 'here we go again!' coming through strong. I knew I was facing another long road ahead. A long road back to good health and happiness. It was coming, a new journey of self-discovery was about to start.

One problem, I couldn't move, I was stuck.

Dead Letter Office

Have you ever felt stuck? Stuck like you're frozen in time and things just aren't moving or happening the way you'd hoped.

Maybe you're stuck in a job you hate, stuck in a relationship that makes you sad or perhaps, as I was, you're stuck in an anxious or depressive loop that's just going round and round and round.

'When you are overwhelmed, tired and stressed, the solution is almost always . . . less. Get rid of something. Lots of somethings'.

Unknown

Years ago, I read an article about something known as the Dead Letter Office. I had no idea what it was; I didn't even realise it was thing. Now it makes perfect sense, *of course* there is a place that all the undeliverable mail goes to rest!

Basically, it's the Postal Mail Recovery Centre, a facility where undeliverable mail and parcels are sent because they have illegible addresses, outdated information or items that couldn't reach their intended recipients. I can only imagine some of the stuff that ends up there!

It didn't sound particularly exciting to begin with but the more I've thought about it, the more I am enamoured with the idea. And now I think I want to work there!

I'd be like a detective in the movies, rummaging through the evidence, eating doughnuts and drinking coffee, trying to reunite people with their lost packages.

I reckon there are all sorts of connections between the Dead Letter Office and humans. Some of it beautiful, some of it sad.

A place of lost communication. Untold stories. Tales of missed connections. Unfulfilled promises. Love letters never reaching their intended recipients. Apologies left unspoken. News of Joy. News of sorrow.

Dead Letter Offices must be crammed full of mystery, ideas, emotions, fears, hopes, ambition, worry, love, disappointment, opportunity, rejection, fun, possibility, beauty, kindness, anger . . .

All stuck. All frozen in time.

Exactly how I was feeling.

Let me go back to something I said earlier. I love the whole idea of the Dead Letter Office; I would love to work there. I guess the goal each day would be to reconcile and reunite items with their rightful owners or ensure they don't go to waste. And in the process have the privilege to see and even feel some proper special moments!

Maybe I could help others to find *their* 'package' of support . . .

I imagine it takes real effort and patience to process the neglected or unaddressed elements, joining the dots of unexplored emotions, untold stories, memories unspoken or buried.

I was in need of a trip to the Dead Letter Office of my mind. I needed to unpick what was going on in my head, work through my thoughts and feelings, working out why I was feeling the way I was feeling. I had to find solutions, I craved answers.

And of course, as many of us know only too well, it takes real effort and patience to process the neglected or unaddressed elements in our heads too. But if we don't, as I was learning – again – things go wrong.

I knew what had triggered me, but couldn't grasp the extremity of what I was experiencing, I didn't know why I was feeling like this, or where/when I would indeed find the answers I needed. I wondered if I ever would.

But the Dead Letter Office is a place of hope and potential. For rediscovery, for reflection, for what once was, what could have been and what might be.

But I was lost. Deep down I knew I wanted to be full of hope and potential again. I longed to rediscover and reflect on what once was, what could have been and what can still be!

But when you feel broken, it feels unachievable, impossible even.

I think there is real beauty in a Dead Letter Office. The letters, once filled with urgency, now rest in collective silence. Imagine the stories that never unfolded, conversations that never transpired and the connections that were left unmade.

A sanctuary for the unsaid.

Unreal amounts of human connection that is lost in the vast expanse of time and space. And in many ways, it's beautiful.

But it's also sad.

Life, much like the undelivered letters, is an intricate blend of missed opportunities and unexplored possibilities. Many of which we may not have known a single thing about.

The Dead Letter Office for me serves as a reminder of the importance of seizing the moment, expressing our emotions and cherishing the connections we have. And acceptance of it all, even when things feel shit or weird and life isn't going the way you'd hope.

It makes me think about the impact of words left unspoken. If there was ever a time on planet earth we needed more people to talk, to share and to connect, my goodness it's right now.

'If we don't tell people how we feel, how will they know?'

Anon

I guess nowadays, in the digital age, The Dead Letter Office is also a metaphor for the virtual spaces where messages remain unread, emails go unanswered and sentiments linger in the digital ether.

It makes me think I need to try harder to embrace the time I have and the profound significance of the words and emotions I choose to share, both professionally and personally.

Maybe there are things that aren't meant to be said, emotions that aren't meant to be shared but bottling it all up doesn't help anyone. Acceptance is key. Acceptance that this is where you are in life and this is how you are feeling, right now. And in time, things will get better. Things will shift, the darkness will lift and you will find you once again.

Dead Letter Offices don't only serve a practical purpose, the official line is that they contribute to the **'preservation of personal connections and historical documentation'**.

Your personal connections are yours, protect the ones that matter, the ones who love, listen, support, lift and see you. The others? Send them to the Dead Letter Office of your mind. Don't let them get stuck but instead pick through them, join the dots, process those unresolved thoughts and emotions, let them rest and set yourself free.

Your story, your journey. This is who you are, creating your own history each and every day. Preserve it.

Think of your Dead Letter Office as a 'mental greenbelt'. A mental space for processing unresolved matters that allows for emotional release, self-reflection and personal growth. By consciously choosing a healthier mental landscape, we open the door to a more balanced, serene and fulfilling life.

Try and Decide

Decision making is seen as a must-have skill in life and in this bonkers world there are two types of decision makers.

There's my wife, the gunslinger. She makes the decisions so fast you can blink, and you'll miss it. The thing needs doing, it shall be done, now. Not now but NOW!

At the other end of the spectrum, there's me, the flounder. The thing needs doing, it shall be done, another day. Maybe not another day soon, but another day EVENTUALLY!

In my journey through the world of personal and professional development, alongside my own mental health struggles, there's a phrase I've encountered more times than I can count: 'I'm trying to be happy'.

I used to believe, like many others, that the solution was simply to try harder, do more, and happiness would follow. I wasn't finding happiness; I was chasing it. And in my relentless pursuit, I realised I had to shift my thinking. I'd become a happiness try-hard, exhausting myself in every way imaginable. I had to change my attitude.

Trying to be happy is like chasing a rainbow, it seems beautiful, but it's always just out of reach, it's elusive. I kept experimenting with new things, different techniques, searching for what would bring me joy. But the harder I tried, the more I found myself stuck in a loop of endless searching without ever finding.

Then came a game-changing realisation; not deciding to *be* happy, but deciding to *allow* happiness into my life. I didn't decide to be happy, I decided to be positive. I just needed to work it out and get good at it . . . soon.

There's no time to be a flounder when your own happiness is concerned. It's not about waiting for circumstances to change, it's about cultivating a mindset. *Deciding* means committing to positive actions and thoughts, practising gratitude, embracing kindness and focusing on personal growth.

'If you want to make the wrong decision, ask everyone'.

Naval

Sure, in the 1300s, as they tried and tried again, Robert the Bruce and his spider pal embodied the timeless truth: perseverance is crucial. But beyond the struggle lies a pivotal choice, being open to happiness. While *trying* reveals our path, *deciding* to embrace joy transforms our daily experience.

So, I decided to let happiness in. But there was more, it was like the floodgates opened . . .

I decided to be open to help.
I decided to embrace contentment.
I decided to accept my quirks.
I decided to let go of negativity.
I decided to say no to things that make me unhappy.
I decided to say thank you to the people who show up for me.
I decided to let go of people who aren't good for me.
I decided to allow feelings to flow, not edit or judge them . . . just feel them.
I decided to focus on being healthy but not compare myself to others.
I decided to embrace this feeling of being lost.

Choosing to let happiness into our lives empowers us to find contentment in the present and live it every day with gratitude.

After a genuinely unreal experience that seemed to absorb all of me, I decided to work on finding the shit that really matters once again.

I decided to be confidently lost.

Every Brilliant Thing

I love the Edinburgh Fringe Festival. I have performed in it many times and I enjoy nothing more than finding new shows to go and see each year.

In 2023 I saw no shows. None. I couldn't, I was in the thick of my darkest days and I couldn't leave my house.

Fast forward 12 months. August 2024 and feeling so much better, I saw a show called *Every Brilliant Thing*. A beautiful, heartwarming one-man show that explores mental health through the power of hope and humour. The story begins with a seven-year-old boy who, faced with his mother's depression, starts a list of 'every brilliant thing' worth living for to share with her.

What starts as a small gesture, a simple collection of things like 'ice cream' and 'water fights', grows into a lifelong pursuit of joy. As the list expands, so does the boy, navigating love, loss and life's rollercoaster.

This isn't just theatre, it's not just a performance, it's a celebration of resilience. The audience is invited to engage, playing roles in the protagonist's journey, making every performance unique, raw and electric. Through the light of everyday wonders, dancing, laughing, vinyl records, the show masterfully tackles heavy topics like suicide and depression with sincerity and levity.

The genius of *Every Brilliant Thing* lies in its simplicity. At its core, it's about connection. It's about how one person's simple act of optimism can ripple outwards, reminding us that even in our darkest moments, there's always a reason to keep going.

When I was a kid, no matter what bug or virus anyone seemed to have, a bottle of old-school Lucozade (in the orange foil wrapper) and a bunch of grapes were the order of the day. I can remember my Gran telling me there was nothing better.

Every Brilliant Thing for me is effectively mental Lucozade and mind grapes, uplifting and real, a vibrant testament to the human spirit, it's a love letter to resilience, joy and the countless brilliant things that make life worth living.

I feel like I was meant to see this show. I feel like the time was right. I feel like I will be thinking about it for a long time. It confirmed that I was writing the right book at the right time.

Until this point, it was like I had been stuck in a John Lennon song. He sang;

> *How can I go forward if I don't know what way I'm facing?*
> *How can I go forward when I don't know which way to turn?*
> *How can I go forward into something I'm not sure of?*

My dark, lonely path back had been lit by many glimmers along the way. I made a note of them as I went.

Below is the very list that I made on my phone throughout my experience. I hadn't even realised I had been keeping my very own list of every brilliant thing. These were my answers to John Lennons questions. My very own mental Lucozade and mind grapes!

Gav's Mental Lucozade & Mind Grapes

Cuddles	The smell of fresh bread
Listening to music	Trampolines
Potato croquettes	Sorrento
Flumes	The greatest showman
A new notebook	Castles
Billy Connolly	Stretching
Crisps	Freddie Mercury
Laughing	Tractors
Ice-lollies	Balloons
Cats	Bunk beds
Detectorists – The TV show	Bobsleighs

Dim sum

Walks with Ali

Walks with Kev

Walks with Jason

Walks with Ewan

Sunkicks

Fresh bed covers

Jumping in to an ice-cold pool on a hot day

New car smell

Fire pits

Crayons

Good coffee

Fresh snow

Ordering another starter instead of dessert; starter, main, starter

Collecting shells

The smell of Christmas

A perfect high five

Olives

Making a cup of tea for Ali

Large pasta

Swings

Hotels

Transformers

Scotland winning at rugby

Fuzzy felts

Stripey door handles

Red squirrels

The very hungry caterpillar

Scooters

Forward rolls

Party sausage rolls

Space hoppers

Comfy sofas

Cottage cheese

Lilos

Scotland

Kwenchy kups

Sloths

Toasties

Heated car seats

Sesame street

Diluting juice

Leaf blowers

Potato croquettes (not the fancy ones)

A Place in the Sun – The TV show

Viva Las Vagus!

Glimmer hunting. It's the new Pokémon. Pokémon hunting for mental health. Except you don't 'gotta catch em all!' The odd one here and there is all you need!

Catching those elusive glimmers tunes you into micro-moments of Ventral Vagal energy, the holy grail of groundedness and connection.

I once heard the vagus nerve described as the body's own messenger pigeon, flying between brain and body. When it goes the wrong way, it can be awful, but we're wired to hunt for danger. We need to survive, and safety cues matter too.

The very same nerve that kicks our ass can be the ultimate chill pill. The human body is a walking contradiction, but we can hack into that and make the most of it.

Remember, glimmers are the breadcrumbs of bliss, even fleeting moments can flip the switch on your vagus nerve, telling your body, 'We're alright'.

Small things can light folks up in a big way. It's science backing up the wisdom of 'stop and smell the roses'. It's like our brains are actually programmed for joy, if we'd only let them.

Who knew?

'The comeback is personal. It's an apology to myself'.

Unknown

And that is where the magic happens; joy! Studies show that the relentless hunt for happiness can actually backfire, leaving us feeling empty or isolated. But joy? Joy is raw, immediate and transformative. It's not a destination; it's a spark, a burst, a wild reminder that life is here to be felt, not solved.

Embracing life's micro-joys and celebrating these fleeting moments rewire us to embrace positivity without the pressure of a finish line. And who knows, maybe the clouds and the trees and the flowers love looking at you too.

Sometimes small, sometimes minuscule, glimmers are always lovely. But sometimes, just sometimes, glimmers become an adrenaline shot to the soul and when you catch them, they catch you.

Those, my friends, are some profoundly meaningful words to conclude Chapter 1. Indeed, this book likely owes its existence to seven of them in particular. So, let's honour them by closing this chapter with the reverence they deserve, as if they were the heart of the most mind-blowingly inspirational, utterly life-changing, deeply thoughtful and majestically relatable piece of non-fiction you've ever read.

When you catch them, they catch you.

Glimmer Tracker

Here's the deal. Every day this week, you're gonna spot one thing – just *one* – that makes you grin like a wally, snort with laughter, or mutter a wee 'Wow' under your breath like you've just seen a double rainbow over a Greggs.

Keep it small. Keep it lovely. Keep it daft. Keep it real.

A pigeon strutting like it owns the street? That counts.

A crisp the size of your face? Absolutely.

The smell of toast that reminds you of your gran's house? 100%.

Write it down. Scribble it. No moment is too silly, too weird or too 'what even is that?'

These are your glimmers, treat them as tiny rebellions against the grind. Micro-miracles. Wee bursts of 'still got it' in a world that sometimes forgets its sparkle.

You're not chasing joy here. You're *catching it off guard*.

So go on. Clock it. Claim it. Sunkick it.

One glimmer a day. You in?

Day	My Glimmer	Why It Mattered
Mon		
Tues		
Wed		
Thurs		
Fri		
Sat		
Sun		

CHAPTER 2

No One Gets Left Behind

T

he world is fucked!

Ok, it's *not* fucked, yet I reckon we can all agree the Netflix documentary about this timeframe is going to be so unbelievably stupid.

The world is of course incredible, there's so much love, wonder, joy, creativity and kindness. And it's everywhere.

But it *feels* a bit fucked. And that matters. It matters because how *you* feel matters and right now it feels like the world has lost a lot of the stuff that makes us feel alive. When those essential things seem lost, we feel lost. Sometimes, it even feels like we've gone missing from our own lives. And that's scary.

When things start to feel overwhelming or uncertain, that love, wonder, joy, creativity and kindness can seem distant, like they're slipping away. Especially with so many human faces buried deep in their phone screens these days, doomscrolling, absorbing the chaos of the world, while the absolute magnificence of life races by unnoticed.

'*Money no longer works for us. We work for it. Money has taken over the world. As a society, we worship and venerate a commodity that has no intrinsic value, to the expense of all else. What's more, our entire notion of money is built on a system which promotes inequality, environmental destruction and disrespect for humanity*'.

Mark Boyle

Not only does the world feel like a shitshow, but it also feels like it's being run by power-hungry, narcissistic grandads, hell-bent on destroying everything that's magical about it for future generations. Miserable, elderly men orchestrating global affairs from under their cosy blankets, behind the walls of their retirement forts, lining their pockets, leaving the rest of us feeling out of sorts.

And it's utterly exhausting, draining even. It's not like we've all got enough shit going on without the GROAN-ups playing real-life battleships!

It's crazy how we go through childhood believing that the world is protected by proper responsible adults and those very same grownups set the rules to bring the structure that keeps us safe, only to grow up and discover that most of them don't have a clue what they're doing!

It can feel like a lot of people just don't give a shit anymore. The world often feels in need of a great big hug. I say get all these Grandads into a special care home for leaders and send for the Grans!

I'm proposing a Global Cuddle Committee. The GCC. Organised and chaired by Grans, tasked with diffusing tensions and fostering understanding through the universal language of hugs and home baking. Their mission would involve bringing world leaders together for warm embraces and cake, turning conflicts into sweet cuddle sessions, navigating disagreements with empathy and custard creams, therefore promoting a more compassionate approach to international relations.

'I wish the women would hurry up and take over'.

Leonard Cohen

Our committee slogan will be 'When in doubt, Hug it out!'. It's *still* diplomacy, just with a softer touch!

Even science tells us that hugs are good for us! They contribute to lower blood pressure, they promote a sense of security and believe it or not, connection! Easy, that's everything sorted then, right? Hugs + Grans + Cake = World Peace and Happiness. Done, thanks for reading my book . . .

If only it was that simple.

Maybe it is that simple?

Is it that simple?

'How wonderful it is that nobody need wait a single moment before starting to improve the world'.

Anne Frank

When the world is on edge, people are on edge. I am always in awe of those who take to the streets (peacefully, obvs) and stand up for what they believe is right, specifically those who want a kinder, fairer, happier, more equal world.

It's like we need the complete opposite to what/who we currently have in power across the globe. Grans would be a good start. Kids too, get *them* round the table! Imagine how good five-year-olds would be at sorting the grownup shit out! A game of Helicopter Tig or Hide 'n' Seek sorts everything. Their energy alone would make a difference. But that would require our world leaders to be vulnerable, present and open to opportunity. It would require them to let go . . .

But if we *were* to go for the literal exact opposite, then it would need to be something/someone young, but also not an actual human.

So, what exactly is the opposite of an old, angry, divisive, power-hungry human?

Someone young, happy, playful, content and fulfilled. A unifying, non-human.

Elmo.

Yeah, Elmo.

Elmo Monster, from *Sesame Street*.

You're possibly now questioning me on the surname there. Trust me, it's his name. But he's no monster! He could save the world with his infectious optimism. Imagine Elmo leading the modern world, his levels of enthusiasm, hope and joy would be infectious, talk about ripples of positivity! Actually, scrap that, tidal waves! His ability to see the good in everything and everyone is second to none, Elmo is the ultimate glimmer hunter, he's pure magic.

I saw the following quote online, it really made me laugh out loud.

'Sesame Street didn't prepare me for any of this shit. Fuck you Big Bird!'

Anon

Fuzzy Logic

I bloody love *Sesame Street*, and it absolutely *did* prepare us for this shit. And yet, here we are. War, poverty, hate, bigotry, corruption, lost hope and a mental health crisis, the likes of which we've never seen in our lifetime.

Sesame Street got it right though. Still does!

For over 50 years a voice of reason, with its laser-like pedagogy, it's bravery to respectfully tackle even the hardest of topics, *Sesame Street* gifted all of us kids a toolbox that cost absolutely nothing! But this was no ordinary toolbox, this one helped us manage our emotions, it kept us curious and filled with wonder. It was the original glimmer machine, teaching right from wrong, delivering sunkicks into our living rooms long before any experts were talking about this.

Perhaps as a kid I didn't appreciate it at the time, but *Sesame Street* was about everything we crave, everything we're drawn to as humans. It was about togetherness. About community. A neighbourhood where everyone is welcome. Real stories. If you watch it today, you'll quickly see how astonishingly, resolutely inclusive the street is. A product of the civil rights movement, from the very beginning, still to this day, it's about diversity and inclusion. Everyone is equal, and unlike so many adults today, it has never *ever* lost its sense of fun.

Today, *Sesame Street* is essentially the exact opposite of many communities, neighbourhoods and countries the world over. I can't imagine what Jim Henson would have made of the world today . . .

He represented *all* humans, even the ones who feel invisible. You can't *not* smile! It's a shining example of how we embrace differences, and that those differences can be surprising and positive.

Its covered everything, and it's delivered in a way that governments the world over just can't seem to perfect; humanly.

Racism, gender, neurodiversity, disability, addiction, climate, mental health and wellbeing, just some of the important themes embraced and delivered through the art of story, play and song.

Story, play and song, from ancient campfires to modern screens, three things we humans have embraced, loved, shared and learned from, for literally *ever*! It's more than a TV show, I'm not exaggerating when I say it is perhaps *the* most iconic TV show ever made.

I can recall the introduction of the character 'Julia' in 2017. Julia is on the autism spectrum. Even in 2017, this was considered a groundbreaking initiative by *Sesame Street* to raise awareness and promote understanding of autism. The goal was simple; foster empathy, reduce stigma and encourage inclusivity. Again, pure magic!

'You are special, no matter what'.

Mr Rogers

Some of you might remember the famous storyline 'Farewell, Mr Hooper' that aired on 24 November 1983. Mr Hooper, who had been a beloved part of the show since the beginning, passed away. The episode focused on the characters learning to cope with the loss of a dear friend, emphasising the importance of remembering and cherishing the memories of loved ones, spotting glimmers along the way.

Dear reader, this is real-life shit helping children and families around the globe. It's such a perfect show that we should all be pretty damn perfect by now.

But we're not.

So, what the fuck has gone wrong? Why are so many of us struggling? Why do so many of us feel on edge? I've already answered this, because the world is on edge. But why is the world on edge?

Humans.

Adult humans.

'There's no "i" in team, but there is an "us" if you jumble it up!'

Bert (Sesame Street)

Did you know, here in the United Kingdom, back in the day, *Sesame Street* was deemed to be 'dangerous' and 'authoritarian'? Get this, some 'experts' suggested that its content was made to change the way kids think and indoctrinate them in some way!

Only the United Kingdom would say and do shit like this.

Or so I thought . . .

Fast forward to today. If some reports are to be believed, certain well-known government representatives in the United States are looking to have it banned. Netflix have already stepped in after Trump pulled funding for the Public Broadcasting Service (PBS), alleging they engaged in 'biased and partisan news coverage'.

Nothing surprises me anymore.

FFS.

I say let's get *Sesame Street* on prescription, for everyone!

Many adults insisted that young kids wouldn't be able to handle its themes. I'll tell you who can't handle its themes, the adults, that's who!

As kids we are nailing it. Then we grow up.

Maybe us adults could learn a few things from the likes of Grover, or Bert and Ernie. Maybe we'd learn that solving problems doesn't always require an overpriced latte and a self-help book . . .

Thinking back to the quote I shared earlier, maybe an 8-foot-2 yellow bird makes for an unorthodox therapist, but even Big Bird knows that embracing your inner child is way cooler than pretending to have your shit together!

Maybe we could take a cue from Elmo and remember that a cheerful 'La la la la, la la la la la!' can instantly brighten your day, even when you're stuck in a meeting with arseholes or goverened by narcissists.

'Keep looking up, that's the secret of life'.

Big Bird

My own kids asked me to describe *Sesame Street* to them. I went with *'a radical, gritty, unafraid of controversy, sometimes psychedelic, avant-garde rainbow of weird and wonderful creatures, with a genuine sort of friendliness and mutual respect among all of them'.*

Sounds like the perfect street to me. A community I feel I can get on board with. I guess this is exactly what I wanted this book to be. A rad, gritty, unafraid of controversy, sometimes psychedelic, avant-garde rainbow of weird and wonderful, with a genuine sort of friendliness and respect about it.

In a world that often leaves people feeling small, rammed full of complexity and grown-up responsibilities, *Sesame Street* is a giant of timeless wisdom. Yes, it's a show for kids, but hidden within those fuzzy Muppet antics and tremendous tunes lies a treasure trove of ageless truths.

There's so much to learn from these felt visionaries, the magic of simplicity, the joy of community, the wonder of curiosity and the power of a rubber ducky to guide us through even the toughest of days. Glimmers, they're there, they're all around us if we just lift our heads up and be open to them.

And kindness. EVERYTHING is about kindness.

'I really do believe that all of you are at the beginning of a wonderful journey. As you start traveling down that road of life, remember this: There are never enough comfort stops. The places you're going to are never on the map. And once you get that map out, you won't be able to re-fold it no matter how smart you are.

So forget the map, roll down the windows, and whenever you can, pull over and have picnic with a pig. And if you can help it, never fly as cargo'.

Jim Henson

I say round up the politicians, the decision-makers and the billionaires. Round up the misogynists, the bullies and the bigots, send them all on a long, *long* walk down *Sesame Street*, and who knows, maybe the next day they'll 'woke' up and smell the coffee!

Literally . . .

Just one thing, did they actually ever tell us how to get (how to get) to *Sesame Street*?

Woke on the Wild Side

Woke up and smell the coffee . . . seriously, that incredible fresh roast smell, ooft, talk about glimmers! Along with the smell of bread, freshly cut grass, a warm day, new cars, Sharpies and babies (yes, babies), the smell of freshly brewed coffee is a true glimmer! Other beautiful smells are available . . . petrol being one of them.

Consider this a woke up call, when we shift our thinking, when we choose to see things differently, even while the world is a mess, then at least we can see it for the beautiful hot mess it really is.

And it *is* a beautiful hot mess!

That's right, I'm talking about embracing the beautiful hot mess of identities and experiences that make us who we are. 'Woke' has become one of those words that gets thrown about by people who don't really understand what it means. It's now seen as a term of abuse, a negative, a slur.

Some of the most powerful and successful people in the world call it the 'woke mind virus'. And now it has been politicised.

FFS!

'I think activism is a part of being young, and it's important that the young show us what their pissed off about. It's not a fad and it's not "wokeism". Can I just say, that gets on my fucking nerves.

They're calling you "woke" if you call out bad things, basically. If you're not racist, you're woke. If you're not homophobic, oh, you're woke. Be woke, kids. Be woke. Be wide awake and fucking call it out'.

Kathy Burke

Woke isn't just a word; it's a call to stand up to ignorance and injustice. It's about challenging what seems to have been accepted as the new societal norms and saying, 'Hey, we can do better than this!'

There is a movement against wokeness. Wokeness is apparently weakness. Well then, to use my favourite unit of measurement once again, I declare myself to be woke as fuck!

Why would one *not* understand that there's not a one-size-fits-all in life? Why would one *not* fight for justice and a fairer society?

'I don't know what word in the English language – I can't find one – applies to people who are willing to sacrifice the literal existence of organised human life so they can put a few more dollars into highly stuffed pockets. The word "evil" doesn't even begin to approach it'.

Noam Chomsky

So, what does it actually mean to be woke?

It's a superpower. A superpower to spot unfairness and discrimination wherever they hide. It's about breaking down the walls of prejudice and privilege and saying loudly, 'We see you, and that's not okay with us!'

But being woke isn't about stirring things up or creating barriers; it's the exact opposite, it's about recognising the power of intersectionality.

What the hell is intersectionality Gav?

Well, I'm glad you asked . . .

Put simply, intersectionality is the concept that all oppression is linked. More explicitly, the Oxford Dictionary defines intersectionality as **'the interconnected nature of social categorisations such as race, class, and gender, regarded as creating overlapping and interdependent systems of discrimination or disadvantage'.**

Intersectionality is the acknowledgement that everyone has their own unique experiences of discrimination and oppression, and we must consider everything and anything that can marginalise people: gender, race, class, sexual orientation, physical ability and so on.

And let's not forget the key action part of this. To be woke is to understand the full injustice. Being woke means getting off your arse and doing something about those injustices you see. Whether it's marching in the streets, educating your peers or calling out your mates when they're acting like fucking dicks towards women!

Sure, being woke isn't always sunshine and rainbows. There are haters lurking around every corner, ready to dismiss you and me as a snowflake or a social justice warrior. But guess what? I'm not here to play it safe or sugar-coat the truth. Like *Sesame Street*, I want to spark a revolution of empathy, compassion and understanding.

So many of us are not okay, and I firmly believe that together we can and should help each other.

But to help, we must see. We must see that all humans are the same. Every face you see in the crowd, every driver on the motorway, every person in the cafe, all of them possess a life as vivid, as intricate and as beautifully messed up as your own. When we grasp this, it's known as Sonder.

Sonder is the realisation that everyone we encounter, whether for a split second or through years of knowing, is a complex universe of thoughts, dreams, struggles and memories.

I shouldn't have to convince you to care about other people. No one should need convincing.

'Yes, I've heard this word. I think sociopaths use it in an attempt to discredit the notion of empathy'.

John Cleese on Snowflakes

This realisation transforms ordinary, fleeting interactions into something extraordinary. The magic of sonder is that it expands your capacity for compassion. It teaches you to look up and see people, to soften. Suddenly, that person sitting across from us on the underground isn't just a background figure. They might be carrying the weight of a recent loss, the joy of a new love or the anticipation of a life-altering opportunity. Their life – like yours – is a constellation of experiences and relationships, none of which we will ever fully grasp.

Sonder reminds you that the world is full of stories, and you're a small, but significant part of it.

'Someday we'll find it, the rainbow connection, the lovers, the dreamers and me'.

Kermit the Frog

It's really not that hard to be a good person. Don't believe the rich fucks when they tell you empathy is the problem. Here's hoping that tomorrow morning more of us *woke* up on the *bright* side of our bed!

A New Hope

As I wrote at the start of this chapter, the world doesn't feel so good just now. These last few years have certainly been challenging and whether it's personal or on a global scale, I don't think there's anyone out there who *hasn't* hoped for things to improve.

I know what it's like to have hope. A full heart, boundless optimism, light everywhere. And I know what it's like to lose it entirely. A heavy heart, an emptiness, a darkness.

With regards to the awful, heartbreaking stories we see and hear on the news, I can't even begin to understand, but I can imagine hope takes on a central role for many.

In tough times, people often wish for things to 'get better soon'. Hope also comes from imagining a brighter future, like getting a new job or finding love. But for some it's dreaming of an end to violence, for peace.

'The more hope you carry in your heart, the lighter it feels'.

Kavya Dixit

I think it should be a world leader's priority to instil hope in humanity but follow it up with real action. As humans we can do so much better. And *we* can definitely help those in charge to change the world for the better, but like most things, it starts at home with ourselves. For the world I definitely hope for peace. For me personally, it's a different kind of peace I hope for; peace of mind.

Hope is a funny old thing, but is it actually good for us?

Over time, hope has been seen differently. Some philosophers, like Thomas Aquinas and Soren Kierkegaard, saw it as crucial for action and spiritual growth.

Others, like Rene Descartes and Friedrich Nietzsche, thought hope was just wishful thinking without real power.

Psychologists started studying hope seriously in the 20th century. In the 1960s and 1970s, they looked at it as a 'positive expectation'. Then, in the early 1990s, Charles R. Snyder introduced his Hope Theory, a big idea in psychology.

His research teaches us that hope is in fact a psychological strength rather than a liability. It enriches every facet of life, enhancing overall wellbeing by fostering happiness, resilience and a profound sense of purpose.

Just before Charles R. Snyder in the 1990s, there was another influential philosopher in the 1980s: Michael Walsh.

In 1985, Walsh and his fellow researchers embarked on a remarkable journey of hope in Astoria, Oregon, after uncovering what appeared to be an ancient treasure map. What followed was a perilous expedition, fraught with life-threatening dangers and terrifying adversaries, including the notorious Fratelli family. Walsh's journey serves as a case study of the transformative power of hope.

This historical, and much-celebrated event, fuelled by hope, underscored several key psychological phenomena: resilience in the face of adversity, the strengthening of social bonds, the significance of unity, and the strengthening of problem-solving capabilities. The successful discovery of the treasure demonstrated hope's critical role in surmounting seemingly insurmountable obstacles, providing definitive support for theories on the psychological and social benefits of hope.

'Don't you realise? The next time you see sky, it'll be over another town. The next time you take a test, it'll be in some other school. Our parents, they want the best stuff for us. But right now, they've got to do what's right for them, 'cause it's their time. Their time, up there. Down here, it's our time. It's our time down here'.

Mikey Walsh

Walsh is renowned for phrases such as 'No one gets left behind' and 'Goonies never say die!' *The Goonies*, as Walsh and his team are known, have become internationally recognised for their involvement in this extraordinary story. Their names – Mikey, Mouth, Data, Chunk, Brand, Andy, Stef and Sloth – are now synonymous with hope. Their unity transformed them into everyday heroes and legends.

Perhaps *The Goonies* should feature in modern-day educational curriculums. Governments worldwide could learn about not only having hope but also sharing it with all humanity. Walsh and his team used the treasure to save a whole town. Being a Goonie has become synonymous with accepting that the real treasure lies within us, in our friendships, curiosity and creativity. Life's greatest rewards are not material but found in personal growth, the bonds we forge, and the memories we create.

In a world that often values conformity, *The Goonies* have taught us to celebrate our differences and honour the misfits among us. They've taught us that hope matters.

Imagine if this was the norm?

'Most people are decent human beings who want to find a way through'.

Richard Osman

So, what else do the scientists actually say about hope? How does Snyder's Hope Theory actually help us in our everyday life? Well, turns out it helps a lot and it's actually pretty incredible.

In terms of mental health, hope empowers individuals to effectively navigate loss, chronic stress and trauma, while bolstering resilience and aiding in mental health recovery.

On a physical level, hope fuels the pursuit of health goals, encourages preventive behaviours and supports adjustment to chronic illnesses.

Moreover, hope's positive influence extends to educational achievement, athletic endeavours, career success, organisational effectiveness and nurturing fulfilling relationships in parenting and beyond.

But it's more than this. Hope radiates beyond individual benefits to enrich communities in profound ways. It inspires altruism and community service, encouraging individuals to actively engage in addressing societal challenges.

And it's *even* bigger still. Hope fosters tolerance and facilitates peaceful conflict resolution, laying the groundwork for harmonious coexistence and collective progress. As a unifying force, hope empowers communities to flourish through shared aspirations and concerted efforts towards a brighter future for all.

You see, hope isn't just a passive wish for better days; it's an active force that propels us forward, even in the darkest times. It transforms adversity into opportunity, and despair into determination. Those who try to extinguish hope may succeed momentarily, but they can never fully drown the human spirit.

For every effort to dampen our dreams, there's an equal and opposite surge of resilience. In the end, hope is what binds us together, fuelling our collective journey towards a brighter, more compassionate world. So, hold onto it tightly, share it generously and watch as it lights the way for you and everyone around you.

'I hope you live louder. I hope you laugh more. I hope you sing at the top of your lungs. I hope you drive with the windows down and let the wind rustle through your hair. I hope you hug. I hope you kiss. I hope you surround yourself with people who make you feel alive. I hope you become the type of person that brings good energy wherever you go, and the type of person people want to be around. I hope you speak what's on your mind, that you raise your voice for injustice, that you tell others that you love them, instead of waiting until it's too late. I hope you live louder, shine brighter. From this moment on'.

Marisa Donnelly

Hope isn't a wildcard; it's essential, like sleep, oxygen and all the things vital to human life. It's just unfortunate that some people out there don't get it and feel the need to spoil it for everyone else!

No Dickheads Allowed

None of us are perfect, accept it! We've all said and done things that are rude, offensive, hurtful and unkind. You have most definitely been a dick at some stage of your life, and I too, on occasion, have been a total dick.

Whether we mean to or not is key. Imagine a scenario where you are an accidental dick, we've all been there, unintentional dickheadedness happens to everyone, everywhere.

There's no 'I' in team, but there's always a dickhead, which does happen to have an 'i' in it!

'No Dickheads Allowed' should be the number one rule in every workplace. It should be written above the door! Just write in Latin and no one will know. When they ask, just tell them it says, 'Be brave'.

In fact, I think the first question at interview should be 'Are you a dick?'. Oh, and hook everyone up to a lie detector test.

> **Interviewer:** Thanks for coming today, are you a dick?
>
> **Candidate:** No!
>
> ***needle goes crazy on the paper***
>
> **Interviewer:** Sorry, I'm going to have to ask you to leave. Only good people can work here, bye dick!

In my head that's how it would work . . .

An audience member challenged me on this recently. Their point wasn't that they thought it was a bad idea, more that a dickhead doesn't know they're a dickhead.

Aye they do. Dicks absolutely know they're dicks.

Imagine we had such a thing as a public volume knob and we could just turn people down in our heads whenever we wanted to? A public volume knob to turn down the nobs!

Unfortunately, we don't have that level of mind control just yet, but we do have a choice. We can accept their dickhead behaviour, or we can challenge their dickhead behaviour. There is always a third option; if you can't change the people, change the people. Remove them from your life. We'll look at this in more detail later.

'The world is full of horrible things that will eventually get you and everything you care about. Humour and laughter is a universal way to lift your head up and say: "Not today you fuckers"'.

Sir Billy Connolly

What Did You Do to Save the World Today?

At one of my events, from the stage I asked the audience what they're doing to save the world. One gentleman responded immediately and said, *'It's not my job to save the world'*.

Then he told me that I'm *'one of them happy clappy types'*. He doesn't know yet that I'm just the happiest depressed person he's ever met.

I explained to him that I'm really not the happy clappy type. I told him I have to dig deep and work bloody hard to not only see and feel the positives in life but to find them in the first place. I told him about the magic of glimmers and shared that I'm on my very own hunt for them and when those sunkick moments happen, it's so worth the effort.

His response?

'I can't be bothered with all that pink and fluffy shite'.

I get it. I really do. It takes effort and energy. We need to get bothered. How else are we going to save the world?

It's a big thought! Just the thought of trying to save the world makes me anxious. But the answer isn't as big and scary as you might think.

The world is shaped by the effort we put in. It's easy to get lost in the noise and it's easy to feel like nothing you do matters. But the world needs *you*!

Giving a shit matters. Choosing to care matters. Showing up matters. Kindness matters. Small moves matter.

Pour some kindness and pour it all over nice!

Nice is well, nice. Nice is like a default setting. Smile, nod, agree, don't ruffle feathers. It's safe and easy. It's overrated. It's the easy way out. Niceness feels good, but it fades fast.

Kindness beats niceness. Nice is Kindness without guts. Kindness is choosing to be genuine. Lead with kindness, you challenge others to be better. Kindness sticks. Kindness pushes for something more. It reminds people they are capable.

'There is always a glimmer in those who have been through the dark'.

Atticus

Climate change, wars, inequality, everywhere you look, it seems like we're hurtling towards chaos. Planet earth is cracking at the seams. You might think the only way to fix it is by doing something huge, like planting a billion trees or leading a revolution.

'The thing about chaos, is that while it disturbs us, it too, forces our hearts to roar in a way we secretly find magnificent'.

Christopher Poindexter

But here's the thing, you can't fix it by gluing everyone else together while falling apart yourself. Saving the world begins with you. Saving the world starts with you saving you.

Yeah, you.

You're not going to create change by running on empty. Self-care isn't selfish, it's essential. It's plugging yourself back in when the world drains your battery.

Stop wearing burnout like a badge of honour, because nobody hands out medals for exhaustion. Look after yourself. That doesn't mean bubble baths and spa days (unless that's your thing). It means boundaries. It means saying 'no' without guilt. It means showing yourself the same kindness you pour into others. Because let's face it, if your cup's empty and you've got nothing left to give, you've become part of the problem, not the solution.

Now, let's talk about kindness. Real kindness. Not the fluffy, Hallmark stuff. Not just 'paying for someone's coffee' (though, hey, that's cool too). I'm talking about looking someone in the eye and genuinely seeing them. I'm talking about showing up. Sharing a smile that says, 'I get it, life's a bit shit right now, but you're not alone'. It's powerful. It's contagious. And it costs nothing.

When you start treating yourself with care, something magical happens, your kindness grows bigger, bolder, more authentic. You're no longer giving from a place of depletion, but from abundance. The world doesn't need another stressed out martyr, it needs people who are alive, awake and whole. People who can lift others because they've lifted themselves.

You're not here to just scrape by. You're here to flourish. And in doing that, you become a beacon. But remember what I wrote earlier, saving the world doesn't start with grand gestures or heroic acts. It starts with small, quiet choices. The choice to look after yourself, and the choice to spread kindness like wildfire.

So, let's get to it. Save yourself first, then we can turn our attention to the whole damn world!

Sometimes, Hard Finds You

Early on in my career, I heard the phrase: **'You get to choose your hard'**.

I was able to relate to this. It felt true for every area of my life where I desired change. Whether it was nurturing relationships, losing weight, creating a show, making money or building a business. The idea was simple yet powerful: while life's challenges are inevitable, we have the power to choose which ones we face.

'You get to choose your hard' is still a popular mantra on social media. I've probably shared it more than once, and many of you have likely seen it, usually as part of a longer piece:

'Marriage is hard. Divorce is hard. Choose your hard.

Obesity is hard. Being fit is hard. Choose your hard.

Being in debt is hard. Being financially disciplined is hard. Choose your hard.

Communication is hard. Not communicating is hard. Choose your hard.

Life will never be easy. It will always be hard. But we can choose our hard.

Pick wisely'.

Unknown

I've always liked this quote . . . until recently.

Like, I still get it, I understand the sentiment, and even agree with it, to a point. Hey, it's even helpful at times, its motivating!

But, I don't choose anxiety. I never have. I didn't choose what happened to me, to be crippled by anxiety so severe I couldn't leave my house. I didn't choose to be so affected by my own experiences that I ended up in therapy, relying on antidepressants to get by.

Heather Jauquet argues that 'choosing your hard' '*. . . comes from a place of privilege and the ability to choose. Sometimes, it just isn't a choice. Hard is hard is hard no matter what you choose'.* Heather herself did not choose to have her cancer.

My dad didn't choose cancer. My mum didn't choose cancer. My mother-in-law didn't choose cancer. My uncle didn't choose cancer.

The reality is, sometimes we don't get to choose our hard.

Sometimes, hard finds you. No warning, no invite, just kicks the door in and helps itself to everything.

And when it does, when you're blindsided by something beyond your control, it can be devastating. Life doesn't always give us options. Sometimes, all we can do is face the hard that finds us and fight like hell to survive it.

Sometimes society brings the hard. Especially for those on the fringes.

'The world is cruel, therefore I won't be'.

Anon

Maybe we can all just work hard to eliminate 'the hard'. When it comes to doing the right thing, acts of kindness, helping others and being a bloody good human are the ways forward. Shout it from the rooftops; be heard, show everyone, be seen, influence others, let it be known.

'It's embarrassing that after 45 years of research and study, the best advice I can give is to be a little kinder to each other'.

Aldous Huxley

And together, let's ensure that – in the pursuit of progress – no one gets left behind.

CHAPTER 3

The Cult of Serious

N o one moons each other like they used to. And absolutely no one is talking enough about potato smiley faces anymore. As for the lack of spokey-dokeys, don't get me started!

I'm often mistaken for an adult, because of my age. And then people get to know me and realise fairly fast that I'm not really built for adulting.

Serious question; are any of us?

'Yttttyyyyyyyyyyyyyyyyyyyyyyyyy yyyyyyyyyyyyyyyyyyyyyyyyyyyyyyyyyyyyyyyyyyy yyyyyyyyyyy yyyyyyyyyyyyyyyyyyyyyyyyyyyyyyyyyyyyy yyyyyyyyyyyyyyyyy yyyyyyyyyyyyyyyyyyyy'

Bowie, Gav's Cat, Walking Across the Keyboard

You know what annoys me is when you go round to someone's house, and they make you take your shoes off at the front door. Nine times out of ten they don't even have a bouncy castle!

It's like there's this unspoken rule that adults should be serious and reserved. It's like a giant dampener on our natural exuberance and joy. The pressure to conform can snuff out our true, vibrant selves.

Some might call it 'growing up'. But if that's what constitutes growing up then count me out, sounds shit.

'At some point a new version of the world is forced upon you by adults and all it's magic is explained away'.

Darcy Hudson

I'm saying that now, but I (like many others) have most definitely done some growing up and it 100% ruined a few great friendships along the way. To be clear, I'm not talking about the kind of growing up that involves getting married, having kids and taking on new responsibilities, these parts of my life are a gift. I'm talking about the desire to be noticed, heard, seen and accepted.

The desire to 'make it', 'to be the funny one' and to be 'successful' not only ruined friendships but impacted upon my mental health in a way that I am only now coming to terms with.

Success that costs you your friends, family or your wellbeing isn't success.

Don't get me wrong, I have had an absolute ball, achieved many incredible things and met some of the best people in the world but if I was given the chance to start over, would I do it all again, in the exact same way?

Nope. Not a fucking chance, I would change everything!

'I wish I hadn't worked so hard. When you're driven to work too hard, you actually ignore what matters. People sacrifice their playfulness, their joyfulness being driven by unconscious needs to validate their existence. Play is so important, and joy is so important'.

Gabor Mate

I remember writing and posting an article for LinkedIn about this idea of going back and doing it all differently. Someone came at me and claimed that I must be lying because if I truly wanted to change everything then I have clearly failed. Perhaps my point wasn't clear.

Read the quote above once again. Gabor makes the point better than I ever could and he's exactly right. Too many of us sacrifice our playfulness and joyfulness to validate our existence.

Nearly every 'successful' person I know has faced battles with their mental health in their 30s and 40s. I've lost track of how many grownups I know who've been on their own intense mental health journey.

What do we all share? At some point, we worked so relentlessly that we lost sight of what truly matters.

I missed almost every one of my kid's sports days. There were weeks I was away four or five nights, rarely home in time for dinner, let alone in time to help with it. Then, COVID-19 lockdowns forced me to hit pause and re-evaluate. Thanks to that time, I discovered my new favourite thing in the world: walking my daughter to school.

Occasionally we skipped to school. Occasionally we skipped big, arms waving, knees as high as possible skips.

I'll never forget something my daughter Ellis told me; *'**Skipping is the funnest way to travel**'.*

When was the last time *you* skipped to work? Skipped *at* work. Skipped round the supermarket. Skipped with your friends while holding hands.

Exactly.

Can you skip? Do you even remember *how* to skip? Do it now, I dare you.

Have you ever seen someone skipping and *not* smiling? Didn't think so.

Ellis is right, skipping *is* the funnest way to travel. My other favourites include pedalo, shoulders and flume.

I wonder at what point the cult of serious kicks in, takes over and we no longer see life in the way we used to?

The Boy Who Said Wow

In a world often obsessed with rules, sophistication and perfection, as I have mentioned already, sometimes it's the simplest moments that resonate the most. And I love it when something so magically human happens that it cuts through the bullshit of the very rules, sophistication and perfection we speak of!

There aren't many worlds more layered with rules, sophistication and perfection than the world of classical music.

Let me tell you the true story of an unforgettable evening at Boston's Symphony Hall in 2019, where a single word – just three letters – reminded everyone of these raw human moments.

Now, I wasn't there, and I knew nothing about this until I came across a short news article, and as I read it, and then watched the YouTube video, the hairs on the back of my neck stood. My first thought was 'Yes! This is what my book is about'.

'The earth has music for those who listen'.

Shakespeare

I don't claim to be an expert when it comes to classical music, but my understanding is this was a typical night for the Handel and Haydn Society, known for their exquisite performances of classical masterpieces. The audience, a mix of seasoned music lovers and curious newcomers, settled into their seats, ready to be enveloped by the sound of Mozart's Masonic Funeral Music. The orchestra played with precision, the notes carrying a sombre beauty that held the entire hall in silent reverence.

And then, just as the final note faded into silence, something extraordinary happened. From somewhere in the audience, a young voice broke through the quiet with a single word: 'Wow'.

And it's a proper good 'Wow' too. A heartfelt, wonderous 'WOOOOOOOW'.

The voice belonged to nine-year-old Ronan Mattin, a boy who is largely non-verbal and has autism. Ronan was attending the concert with his grandfather, Stephen, who immediately felt a twinge of concern. Had Ronan's innocent outburst disrupted the performance? What would the audience think?

But instead of discomfort or irritation that one might (wrongly) expect, Ronan's 'WOOOOOOOW' was met with smiles, nods and even a few tears. The musicians on stage paused, touched by the pure, spontaneous reaction. David Snead, the president of the Handel and Haydn Society, was moved by the moment, recognising it as something truly special.

Ronan's 'wow' wasn't just a reaction; it was an expression of something deeper, pure wonder. In that moment, he captured the essence of what music is meant to do. In fact, nah, fuck that, Ronan reminds us of what *life* is meant to do: move us, inspire us and remind us of the beauty in the world. It wasn't rehearsed or polished; it was raw and real. It was the kind of moment that doesn't just happen; it emerges from a place of genuine connection.

The wee guy felt it.

'That's the thing with magic. You've got to know it's still here, all around us, or it just stays invisible for you'.

Charles de Lint

And that's the magic of glimmer moments. They remind us to pause, to feel, and to appreciate the magic around us. That sunkick moment. Whether it's a piece of music, a breathtaking view, or a simple act of kindness, these moments have the power to cut through the noise of everyday life and bring us back to what truly matters. It's not about perfection or protocol, it's about connection, emotion and those rare instances when something truly moves us.

We don't need to be experts to appreciate the beauty of life; sometimes, all it takes is a little bit of wonder and a willingness to be moved.

No one should ever be so grown up, so busy or so serious, that they can't be moved by magic.

'Love it when you're sitting at home minding your own business and then suddenly you hear a flock of honking geese flying overhead, just the most ridiculous little noise briefly injected into your day, always a pleasure'.

Dan Douglas

There are people we meet in life that make everything seem magical. Whether you meet them in real life, or in books, or online . . . cherish them.

To Ronin Mattin, big thanks for the reminder little man.

Stop (Collaborate and Listen)

I wrote a quote down during one of the COVID-19 lockdowns that has stuck with me . . .

'The world is delivering us a slowdown. Whether we want to slow down or not, we get to'.

We had a choice to embrace it, or not. Yes, the world was in chaos, yet we had a chance to stop and notice the stuff that matters most.

Crazy thought . . . what if we saw chaos as a sign that magic was afoot?

Stick with me . . .

Maybe, just maybe, during lockdowns, we got a glimpse of what life *should* be like. Strip away the illness, death and loneliness that so many endured, and we were left with something powerful: togetherness, reconnection, learning to bake, learning to dance, long walks, board games, putting others first. Being.

Indeed, the coronavirus pandemic was described as a 'boom time for boredom'. Apparently, most of us are shit at being shut in our homes indefinitely, even with the internet to distract us. For me it forced a rethink. A reimagining.

I learned my ducks were not quite in the row I thought they were. I didn't even have ducks. I had squirrels and they were in a fucking rhombus, dancing the Hokey-Cokey.

I don't know about you, and you may think this is a bit weird, but during COVID-19 – as bloody awful as it was – I found joy.

And if I can find joy during a pandemic, I knew if I put my mind to it, I could rediscover it in the dark. I just needed to find the light switch, and then maybe, just maybe along the way I would find me . . .

Joshing Around

Let's talk about Josh Swain, the man who turned an identity crisis into the internet's most absurd self-help spectacle. Back in 2021, when most of us were deep in existential dread, Josh decided to take his own 'Who am I?' moment to a whole new level. He messaged a bunch of other guys named Josh Swain on Facebook, challenging them to a showdown: winner keeps the name. The idea? A 'Battle of the Joshes'.

'You're probably wondering why I've gathered you all here today', he wrote one morning to a group of strangers.

'Precisely, 4/24/2021, 12:00 PM, meet at these coordinates' he instructed.

'We fight, whoever wins gets to keep the name, everyone else has to change their name, you have a year to prepare, good luck'.

Another Josh Swain replied, *'Because we all share the same names . . . ?'*

He took a screenshot of the Facebook group chat and posted it on Twitter with the following words, *'there can be only one'*.

In typical internet fashion, the whole thing exploded, culminating in a showdown in Lincoln, Nebraska. Hundreds of Joshes and non-Joshes alike came to witness the battle of pool noodles and chaos. It wasn't just about the name, it was about re-claiming identity.

Josh Swain took all of us on a journey, showing that sometimes, you have to face the absurd to find yourself again. Whether you're a Josh, a Gavin, a Sarah, a whoever or just another person trying to make sense of life, his story screams a lesson: let go, let loose and embrace the ridiculous. The 'Josh Fight' serves as a masterclass in embracing the silliness.

'Don't let other people decide who you are'.

Anon

The winner? Four-year-old 'Little' Josh Vinson Jr.

What started out as a bit of a josh (sorry, not sorry) resulted in thousands of dollars being raised for a local children's hospital and food being delivered to local foodbanks.

So, next time you're lost, don't book a silent retreat, stop searching for meaning in a sea of serious faces. Instead, grab a pool noodle, find your own weird tribe, and throw yourself into the absurdity of self-discovery.

'The ego can exist only if you take yourself and everything seriously. Nothing kills the ego like playfulness, like laughter. When you start taking life as fun, the ego has to die, it cannot exist anymore'.

Rajneesh

Skipping Class

Inspired by Josh, I decided to accept my daughter's advice and embrace the silly.

Filming in Edinburgh during Monday morning rush hour is like stepping into a live-action stress documentary . . . grim faces, fast strides and the collective sigh of a city not quite caffeinated enough.

We asked commuters the funnest way to travel. Plane? Wrong. Bike? Nope. Rollercoaster? Pffft. The answer, obviously, is skipping. Some scoffed, some laughed, some looked at us like we'd just asked them to lick a lamppost in winter. But then . . . magic.

A few brave souls shrugged off the weight of adulthood, took a deep breath and skipped. In suits, in heels, handbags and manbags swinging in the air. And for those few glorious moments, the city softened. Laughter broke through the morning fog, shoulders dropped, and people remembered, playfulness equals joy, movement is fun, travel can be play, and sometimes, the best way forward is with both feet off the ground. We filmed the whole thing, and it was beautiful.

Edinburgh, for a heartbeat, skipped together.

Joyriding

Family (and skipping) aside, I can tell you the happiest I've ever been is at the start of my comedy journey. Before it was even considered a career. It was simply a delight. Writing, rehearsing and performing with my best friends. Winging it. No pressure, no career plans, no outside expectations, no busyness. Just pure fun, making it up as we went along, pure energy, creating something so wildly silly that would, one day, fill massive rooms with nothing but people, laughter and joy.

Back then, we were like kids, full of natural naivety, oblivious to the rules we were breaking. It was pure, unfiltered play. *And*, it was effortless.

Around the same time I first dipped my toe in stand-up, I was doing what almost no other young men were doing; I was becoming a primary school teacher. It was the same year. I was 18.

I discovered quickly that they're the same thing! In a classroom by day, and the clubs by night, my job remained the same; capture the imagination quick, take them on a journey, make them laugh and feel amazing, so much so, they want to come back and see you again.

I loved both. I still do.

I learned a lot in the clubs, but I learned more from the kids. More about humour, more about learning and even more about joy and fun. I learned more about life and living it to the full. All kids are inspiring but kids under the age of 10 take it to another level. The way they turn up for life is mind blowing, they don't just walk into a room, they gallop! And they know what's important.

Kids are naturals at finding joy. They're open to it. They have a natural gift for taking any situation and diving right in, finding the fun, the creativity, the love, whatever magic the moment holds. They're not trying to impress anyone, and the hollow rush of getting a 'like' on Instagram isn't even on their radar.

It's their mindset, their curiosity, their openness, and their incredible ability to show up, embrace everything and just play. Kids are experts at knowing exactly what they need to get out of play. Adults, not so much.

I learned many things, but here are three that have stayed with me since my time as a primary school teacher:

1. **Kids instinctively seek to make everything more fun and exciting.**
2. **They believe that anything is possible.**
3. **They know that the effort is worth it in the long run.**

What do I mean by my third point? It's why they'll spend hours building an epic Lego masterpiece only to knock it down with four bits to go and start over building 'something better', just for fun. It's why they'll race outside to build a den in the garden, even after being told, 'It's going to rain in an hour'.

That last point about the den sums up the whole world for me. Too many adults have made a shift. A shift in their head *and* their heart, from being the type of person who'd run outside to build that den, to being the type who now spends their life thinking, feeling and saying, 'But it's going to rain in an hour'.

How to Cheer Up:

A. Whisper 'beep boop' to yourself.

B. Say 'potato' over and over as fast as you can and keep a straight face.

C. Using your fingers, plug your nose:
   - Say 'sneep snop' in a really high voice.
   - Say 'boopdedoop' in a really deep voice.

D. Finally, say 'bubbles' in the angriest voice you can.

Repeat until not sad!

So, let's revisit those three points through the eyes of a grownup, *you* to be exact:

1. Do you want things to be more fun and exciting? I really hope you do, because the world could do with more fun and excitement right now. Fun and excitement fuel happiness, they ignite joy and a sense of adventure in our lives. And they're good for you! Remember, there is nothing childish about play!

2. Do you believe anything is possible? I hope so, because the world desperately needs belief. It needs new ideas. It needs people to believe things can get better. Granted, it's hard when you've become immersed in the regulated, overthinking, rule-enforced world of the adult! But that belief creates a much-needed optimism, it's infectious, it opens doors and it lifts others.

3. And we all know what 'it'll be worth it in the long run' means, right? It means, in the short term, it might be rough, messy even; here we go again on yet another journey of change and growth. When are we *not* on a journey of change and growth?

I'll take a 5-year-old's view on the world over a 55-year-old's all day long . . .

School Principal: I see a bad egg when I look at your niece. She is a twiddler, a dreamer, a silly heart. She is a jabberbox. And frankly . . . I don't think she takes a thing in her life or her career as a student seriously.

Uncle Buck: She's only six.

School Principal: That is not a valid excuse! I hear that every day and I dismiss it.

Uncle Buck: I don't think I want to know a six-year-old who isn't a dreamer, or a silly heart. And I sure don't want to know one who takes their student career seriously.

If you've never seen it, Uncle Buck is a tremendous film that doesn't belong to any one genre. It is however entirely made up of comedy and heart. Starring the legend that is John Candy, I recommend you give it a go, there are so many valuable lessons. Above all else, it's one of those films that inspires viewers to embrace their flaws and believe in second chances!

Silly Hearts Unite!

I cannot stress enough how important it is to do silly, frivolous things that serve no other purpose than making you happy.

Now, in my mid 40's I have enough life experience to say and do silly things with complete confidence.

'There's power in looking silly and not caring that you do'.

Amy Poehler

I can't decide if I've gotten sillier with age, or more sensible. Maybe both. Could I be both silly and sensible?

Is it sensible to be silly? Or, silly to be sensible? Or, sensible to be sensible? Or, silly to be silly?

Maybe as we get older, something happens to our sense of risk, we become more aware of everything that could go wrong. Maybe we need serious and sensible people when it's difficult and silly people when life's going well.

But there's being sensible and there's being sensible. I want to be on time and remember to take a coat for when it potentially rains. I'm all for serious and sensible to keep me and my family safe, but I never ever want to reach the stage in which I no longer feel alive.

Life *isn't* safe though, it's a wild ride of bad decisions, ridiculous laughter and intense risk. Without the twists, turns and crazy detours, well, there's just boredom left. It's near impossible to light that fire in you when there's a wet blanket on your soul.

As author Danny Wallace says in his bestselling book 'Yes Man', maybe sometimes it's riskier not to take a risk. Sometimes all you're guaranteeing is that things will stay the same.

Serious question time again: Are you having enough fun?

'Too many of us have tried to tone down our weirdness for friends or partners, only to later learn that we were suppressing the best things about us. There's no joy like the joy of being your strange self and finding that there are people who love you for it'.

Anon

According to science journalist Catherine Price, letting loose is not just enjoyable, it's essential for your health and happiness! When you have fun, when you play, says Price, you are more relaxed and more socially connected. True fun contains these three key elements: Playfulness, connection and flow.

'Playfulness, connection and flow all feel great on their own', she explains. 'But when we experience all three at once, something magical happens. We have fun. And that doesn't just feel good, it is good for us'.

Flow is something I talk about a lot on stage. If you're not familiar with the science (see Csikszentmihalyi), then I hope you've at least experienced the feeling. Flow is life turned up to eleven! Life in high definition, it's your brain firing on all cylinders, effortlessly synced with the moment.

It's where your skills and challenges meet in a perfect dance-off, and everything just *works*. Time? Irrelevant. Ego? Gone. Your brain's dropping dopamine and norepinephrine all over the shop, sparking focus, creativity and joy. The boring bits of your brain? Switched off.

Flow is your inner David Bowie kicking in, where effort meets mastery, and your inner Freddie Mercury making life feel raw, powerful and unapologetically real. It's where life feels epic, electric and totally *you*.

Bored AF

I have been involved with events and businesses that take themselves so unbelievably seriously that I had to get out. Zero room for fun, zero room for mistakes and zero room for wellbeing.

I've never fully understood the glamorisation of overworking. Starting at 5 a.m. and not stopping til you drop can piss right off. Hustle culture can do one too, and as for being a lion or a shark, well, that too can well and truly get to fuck!

As someone who has experienced burnout on more than one occasion, I have never been more confident when I say that no job requires you to work so unbelievably hard that you think you might die.

'Take life easily, lovingly, playfully, non-seriously. Seriousness is a disease, the greatest disease of the soul and playfulness the greatest health'.

Rajneesh

I've done it, it's shit, and it doesn't end well. And anyone who tells you it's the only way to succeed is – what we here in Scotland call – a fud.

I've also never fully understood the attraction of *under*working. Turning up on the dot, doing absolutely nothing, getting involved with nothing, bare minimum effort, zero responsibility, no purpose and then leaving on the dot at the other end.

'I am never bored. To be bored is an insult to oneself'.

Jules Renard

As someone who has experienced boreout on more than one occasion, I have never been more confident when I say that no job should ever be so unbelievably boring that you think you might die.

'Boreout' you say Gavin? Well just what in the fresh hell is boreout?!

'Boreout is a state of dissatisfaction and demotivation that a person experiences due to being bored and unchallenged at work'.

Boreout is obviously a play on *burnout*, which as we all know is caused by exhaustion, fatigue etc. from overwork. In contrast, boreout results from not having enough challenging, stimulating or meaningful work.

I'm pretty sure we can all agree that being bored at work can, over time, lead to feelings of apathy and frustration. We can probably all agree that boredom is also quite normal at times and not always a bad thing.

Actually, it's a good thing at times. It's where creativity brews and where the spark of genius can exist. Learning to sit with discomfort, to feel without distraction and to connect with your own self instead of pixels is a radical act of reclaiming your humanity.

Understatement time: **phones aren't helping!**

What would you rather have, a new SMART phone or an extra couple of years?

For many, their phone has become their identity, their comfort blanket and, terrifyingly, their emotional regulator. That's why so many of us reach for it the moment we wake up, even in the middle of the night. But in soothing ourselves with constant stimulation, we're numbing something essential, our ability to truly feel. To just be.

BUT . . .

Research tells us that being *chronically* bored at work can have very damaging consequences and I reckon it's something we need to talk about more!

'One must choose in life between boredom and suffering'.

Madame de Stael

Not only can chronic boredom have detrimental effects on productivity and job satisfaction, but it can also lead to unhealthy coping mechanisms, such as overeating and excessive screen time.

Boredom is not simply a fleeting sensation; it can impact overall wellbeing.

I've already spoken of the silver linings that COVID-19 delivered for me. But it delivered on the business front too!

In the beginning, the panic was real. It picked us up, slapped us about a bit, turned us upside down and gave us a good shake until all our dinner money feel out our pockets.

Then it forced some solid decision-making. My boredom was gone. And then a creativity tsunami followed!

I want to clarify something here; I didn't know I was bored. I do now. I was done. I was ready for pastures new. Nearly 20 years doing my thing, even with all the highs it brings, I was simply fed up.

What I also didn't know was that my boredom was chronic. Sounds a little ridiculous, but it's incredibly serious and affects workplaces across the world now more than ever.

Ruth Stock-Homburg, a professor of management and human resources at the Technical University of Darmstadt, Germany, has identified three main aspects of the boreout phenomenon: **'being terribly bored, having a crisis of growth and having a crisis of meaning'**.

I *was* unbelievably bored. I *was* having a crisis of growth (personally and professionally) and I *was* having a crisis of meaning.

The result?

Stress, anxiety, exhaustion, sadness, loneliness and a distinct lack of creativity.

Weirdly, if you look at these symptoms, and some mentioned previously, it's the exact same results brought about by burnout.

'*Boredom is the price one pays for not enjoying everything*'.

Marty Rubin

Part of the problem here is that usually when someone recognises it, they've already been chronically bored for quite some time.

Lotta Harju of the EM Lyon Business School, France says, '*Boreout is different from burnout in the sense that bored-out employees rarely collapse out of exhaustion. Bored-out people may be present physically but not in spirit, and people can keep doing this for a good while*'.

Learning about boreout has forced me to change my thinking a little regarding how I am feeling at times. Am I burning myself out, or am I actually boring myself out? Both different, both serious, neither ending well. Oh, and both need some attention!

Reflection helps. Particularly reflecting on how certain tasks at work are making you feel. Considering whether you are feeling overwhelmed and drained (burnout) or unengaged and underwhelmed (boreout) can help at times to understand our current situation.

If you're running the risk of boreout and looking to reclaim your spark, talk about it! Seriously, don't just stew in silence. If you're feeling unchallenged or underused at work, have a chat with someone. You might just land yourself some new tasks that actually excite you. Say yes to things outside your usual job description, volunteer for projects, throw your hat in the ring for something different, who knows where it might lead?

And don't just sit around waiting for inspiration to strike, go after it! Proactively seek out opportunities to contribute, shake things up and make a difference. While you're at it, use any downtime wisely, skill up! Take an online course, dive into a workshop or pick up a certification that makes you feel fresh. Oh, and don't forget life outside of work.

The key to staying engaged? A great blend, like a delicious smoothie. Remember your loved ones? Remember hobbies? Mix your time up, work, hobbies, loved ones and whatever makes you feel alive. It's not all about making money or having a side hustle. Not every day needs to be a TED Talk.

When you're having a tough time, ask yourself, am I just bored? If the answer is yes, boot boredom in the dick. Dream, play, explore, reinvent, re-energise and unbore yourself when you need to!

Yes, purpose, adventure and possibilities are all around you. But let me remind you, we live in a great, big, vast world that most of us have seen NONE percent of. And it's absolutely, utterly and beautifully rammed with the most joyfully silly moments that are so worth the time and effort to not just notice but embrace and truly appreciate.

A Sweetcorn Fable

Once upon a time in a town far far away, there lived a young boy.

One morning the young boy's mother was baking a cake for the village fair.

'Mother, Mother' the young boy called from the top of the stairs.

Mother couldn't hear for the sound of her whisking.

'Mother, Mother' the boy called out once again, this time running down the stairs.

Still Mother heard nothing.

The boy ran into the kitchen, 'Mother, Mother, come quick'. Mother turned with a startle.

'What's wrong?'

'You must come now Mother, it's important'.

The boy grabbed his mother's hand and began running towards the stairs. Mother was trying hard to not get flour all over the house.

'This had better be important!' exclaimed Mother.

'It is Mother, it is!' Replied her son.

They ran all the way up the stairs, the boy's energy rising all the way.

'Just what is going on?' Cried Mother.

'Just wait and see Mother, this is simply marvellous!'

They ran all the way along the upstairs hallway and the boy threw open the bathroom door.

'What is it?' shirked Mother

'It's truly one of the most marvellous things I have ever seen' he replied.

The boy pointed directly into the toilet,

'Look Mother, look how much sweetcorn is in my jobby'

By G.M. Oattes

Like all good fables, there is always an important message. In fact, usually three.

1.   Stay excited.

2.   Notice the little things.

3.   Take Pride in all that you Produce.

Always.

Silly Science

Let's face it, life can sometimes feel like a never-ending parade of meh. But before you spiral into existential dread, let's consult an expert; your inner goofball. Yes, that untamed, unapologetic side of you that snorts at bad jokes, farts and does air guitar solos in the kitchen.

'This morning I was saying that I made a super tight schedule for myself this week, to make sure I get everything done, and my daughter said, "Make sure you get weird and take some dance breaks".

So I offer you this to you: Make sure you get weird and take some dance breaks'.

Maggie Smith

National Goof Off Day is an actual thing and it's exists to remind us: *Stop. Take a breath. Be ridiculous.* Goof Off Day isn't just a calendar gimmick, it's a public service announcement.

Research backs this up, humour and silliness are psychological magic wands. According to Dr Nick Kuiper, humour creates distance from negativity, reframing even the nastiest curveballs as opportunities for laughter. Translation? No need for kale and yoga, when life gives you lemons, wear them as hats, and call yourself 'Madame Citrus'.

I mean, making lemonade is fine too, just not nearly as fun!

When you're stuck in traffic or drowning in spreadsheets, ask yourself: *What would a five-year-old do?* Then do it. Blow a raspberry, hum a silly tune or shout, 'BOGIES' as loud as you can! The world's crazy enough, why not meet it with a little silliness of your own?

I'm tired of being an adult and I'm considering stepping down.

So, to finish this chapter, let's put all this to the test and fully embrace something so silly it's majestic. Allow me to set you a challenge.

The challenge: Eat an orange in the shower.

Yup, you heard, eat an orange in the shower.

WTAF Gav?

Ok, hear me out. This is something I overhead on the train. At least I think I overheard it, there's always a chance I dreamt it, but it is pure joy. A little chaos with no mess. Silliness with no sticky hands. A simple pleasure without having to worry. A tiny act of rebellion against routine. The aroma from the orange being intensified by the steam. Just you, your bare self and the juice from the orange. You peel it, you take a bite, shove it in your mouth, and you can let it go. Pure bliss, a juicy moment in a serious day.

Do yourself a favour, buy/pick an orange.

Shower.

CHAPTER

Is This All We Are?

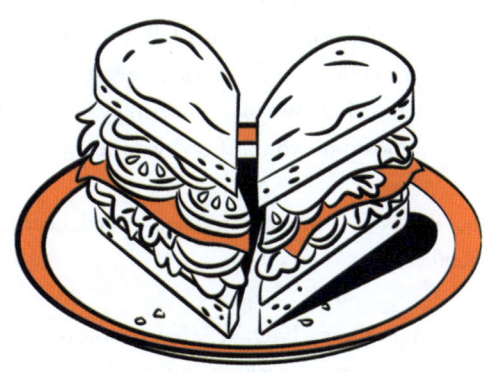

I remember as a young kid being obsessed with sticker albums. It was so exciting when my dad brought home the latest one, the buzz of going to the wee shop to get packets of stickers, only to tear them open was just pure magic. The goal was always to fill the album as quickly as possible, so I was first to be able to say 'completed it!'.

The race was always on.

We would spend every ounce of our pocket money, no matter how little we had, on those stickers. It's an expensive business! More often than not, it was football stickers. I don't even like football. But like millions of other wee kids, I was obsessed with collecting these sticky treasures. From the highs of finding a 'Shiny' to the crushing lows of discovering your pal had a 'doubler' of the sticker you needed most but wouldn't do 'swapsies' with you. It had it all.

Every day at school it was the same mantra; need, need, need, got, need, need, need, need, got, need . . .

I never completed a single album. Ever. Very few people did. Sticker collecting was a short-lived fad for many, or we kept getting the same stickers over and over. The 'swap' pile grew, and the elusive glittery ones remained out of reach. It became repetitive, frustrating, boring even. Distractions crept in, jealousy flared, others completed their collections first, and plus their parents bought them more stickers. So, we moved on to something else.

There were always rumours that someone had completed it. Never saw any proof so in my head it didn't happen. I reckon no one ever truly completes a sticker album. I really wanted to though, more than anything, was that too much to ask?

So often I wished I'd never started!

The attic in my mum's house most likely has a box of nearly completed sticker albums. Everything from World Cups to Transformers to the Olympics. I even had the Neighbours album. None of them full. I'm pretty sure I still have a shiny Helen Daniels.

The shiny's are great, but it's all the other stickers that make the album feel full.

Life is a lot like those sticker albums, no one ever completes it. It's like the internet, you can't finish it, there's simply too much to do, too much to see. Yes, life is full of glittery prizes but there's just too many 'shiny's' to collect. And it always feels like there's someone who has nailed it and has it all. They've 'completed it!'

'Sometimes the grass is greener because its fake'.

Anon

But that's part of the problem for so many. It's always been the problem. The race is on, a constant search for the big prize of being first, constantly seeking the glittery moments, craving what others have, the next big thing, the dream car, the promotion, the mansion, prepared to swap it all just to be the first to say 'completed it', and then probably post it on Instagram.

Yet another chorus of need, need, need . . .

In life, the things we think we need are usually things we want. We really don't need very much. Again, the shiny's are nice, but that's not what fills us up.

The only finish line in life is death and I'm not sure about you but I'm definitely not keen on finishing. There's so much to learn and so much to do, you can't possibly do it all. By all means, ram your life full and live life to the max but one of the biggest lessons we can learn is to be grateful for what/who we *do* have rather than spend all our time thinking about what we *don't* have.

I'm just like you are. I enjoy collecting experiences, new memories and (sometimes) making new friends.

And if you're one of *those* types, always chasing the next big shiny prize then there's no shinier prize than your happiness. And we all know the things that make us happy aren't things.

Here's to being happily unfinished.

Buffering

Have you ever questioned your existence?

I've come to realise I do it a lot. Life can often feel like a relentless series of tasks and obligations. Every day a mini life. We're born, get up, go to work, manage our responsibilities, come home, chores, tired, retire. And then we repeat it, over and over, day after day. And then we die.

It's easy to find ourselves asking, 'Is this all we are?'.

'A resume is a mounting collection of evidence that your childhood never existed . . . it's a reverse bucket list of shit'.

Darby Hudson

Every generation wrestles with the same question. We are, undeniably, creatures of habit but our lives aren't just a countdown of years, a resume of work experience or a tally of possessions.

Our lives are defined by the impact we make, the joy we share, the love we give. When we inspire, when we uplift, when we break down the barriers between us, we touch the very core of what it means to be human.

Remember when you were a child, staring up at the night sky, eyes wide with awe, every single star a glittering possibility. Or if you're anything like me, staring into the massive freezer in the local shop with the most magical selection of ice-lollies and ice-creams you'd ever seen, every single one a glittering possibility! *That* right there is the pure essence of our humanity, a relentless curiosity, an unquenchable thirst for the unknown (or frozen juice). That wonder is a powerful reminder of what it means to be truly alive.

Maybe we're too busy focusing on what we *think* matters, rather than the stuff that *really* matters. We're humans, we're designed to copy, to follow, and maybe, just maybe – probably definitely – thanks to an out-of-date education system, smart phones and the invention of social media, we're witnessing, following and copying the wrong behaviours . . .

Don't Let the World Make You Normal

Let's be honest, the world isn't going to change to accommodate you. If you're waiting for everything to fall into place, for that perfect moment, and only then will you start living your best life, you'll die waiting.

'Don't ask yourself what the world needs. Ask yourself what makes you come alive, and go do that, because what the world needs is people who have come alive'.

Howard Thurman

The modern world is nothing short of spectacular. Yes, I understand the news can be horrendous, old angry men are fucking it up, social media can piss us off, and nostalgia can make the past seem rosier. But I make a real effort to *not* buy that perspective. I said the modern world is 'spectacular', not 'perfect'.

Despite the challenges modern life throws our way, we have countless opportunities to be reminded of what matters and to enhance our wellbeing. We're not meant to confine ourselves to our rooms, glued to screens. We're not meant to be isolated. We're not meant to fill our bodies with shit that's not actually food, or with sugary drinks. We're not meant to stay still.

We're built to move, run, jump, dance and play. We're meant to embrace the outdoors and do roly-poly's down hills. We're meant to learn and create. We're meant to connect, to protect communities and be part of a vibrant movement.

We're meant to savour incredible natural foods and drink delicious fresh water. We're meant to explore new places, walk in the rain, see sunsets, meet inspiring people and immerse ourselves in diverse cultures. We're meant to marvel at art in all its forms and let it move us in ways we never imagined.

We're built to grow, to get better and to seek out the beauty in the world around us. There are journeys to be had, we're made to travel far and wide, taste the world's flavours, meet its amazing inhabitants and to express ourselves through our own creativity.

The modern world is an open invitation to live fully, to embrace every moment, to laugh so hard it hurts, to hear music that changes our lives, to have our minds blown and to find joy in the extraordinary rainbow of life.

What's really cool, is that right now, whatever your age, you can start to build the world you want for you. Unfortunately, for many years, humans haven't always got this right. We have in so many ways got it very wrong.

And the result is a tiredness. An unhealthyness. An anger. A mental *ill*-health. And again, many of us are left asking; is this all we are?

'Your diet is not only what you eat. It's what you watch, what you listen to, what you read, the people you hang around . . . be mindful of the things you put in your body emotionally, spiritually and physically'.

Anon

But take a closer look at the world. There's a vibrant energy waiting to be discovered. A sense of good health and mental wellness. Almost no one wants war. Almost everyone welcomes kindness. There's magic. Sometimes we must dig deep to find it, but it's there, all around you.

And guess what? You have every right to be inspired by it, to learn from it, to soak it all in, to contribute to it, to be a part of it, to be led by it and even to lead it. There's always time to chill. There's always time to scroll. There's always time to stop and do nothing, sometimes we need to! But it's too easy to fall into that routine all the time.

Sitting in your comfies, basking in the glow of your phone for hours on end won't get you to where you want to be. That's not the light that will light the way forward when you don't know which way you're facing. You've already worked out that the weeks are getting faster, time stops for no one.

Look, I'm pretty sure you're switched on to this stuff. You probably look after yourself more than you give yourself credit for. But too many of us are tired, bored, fed up, stressed, sad, anxious, angry.

I can assure you though, there is a solution and it's not complicated.

No, it's not a Red Bull on the way to work. Or a Monster to get you through your day. It's way healthier than that. Your body and brain are not built for those drinks, hence the reason you would die if you drank too many of them.

When I say the solution isn't complicated, it really isn't. In fact, it's dead obvious. It doesn't have to cost loads of money, but it will cost time and energy. Better still, you're built to do it all . . .

All Good Things Come in Fours

Seasons, elements, chambers of the human heart, the four immeasurables of Buddhism, four-leaf clovers and perhaps the most fab four of all, John, Paul, George and Ringo, sometimes we need four of something for an entirely different something to truly click . . . for magic to happen.

Tomatoes + garlic + basil + parmesan = actual deliciousness. Or actual Bruschetta, depending on how you spell it. Whack that on toast and you're in heaven. Toast usually has that effect, sourdough in particular.

Ok, I've gone on yet another food glimmer tangent! I'll come back to food in a little while.

Sometimes it can feel like life is all about surviving, when things are a bit shit, it's about getting through the week, one day at a time. Don't get me wrong, sometimes it needs to be that way and sometimes it is *literally* about surviving.

'What you do frequently becomes your frequency'.

Anon

But we're allowed to be more than just surviving. We are allowed to crave more. We are allowed to want more, for ourselves, for our loved ones and for the world around us. Maybe most importantly, we are allowed to demand more, from ourselves, from society and from the universe. We have the right to aspire and the more I embrace my own glimmer journey, the more I find profound opportunity for personal growth and enrichment.

Many books out there explore the classic self-help trinity of mind, body and spirit. Perhaps, depending on your own interpretation, this book is no different, but let's go bigger! One bigger to be exact. Who needs a trinity when there's a worthy quaternity (nope, I'd never heard this word before either) alternative, a simple quartet that's less about what makes you happy, and more about what makes you feel alive? A *four*some foundation upon which moments of real magic are crafted and memories are made.

Call them what you want, the Beatles, the Fantastic Four, the Golden Girls, your very own Teenage Mutant Ninja Turtles, I assure you there is nothing petite about this four!

Let me introduce you to the pillars that, for me, underpin the entire concept of life and remind me why it's so fucking good to be alive. That's right, in case you haven't guessed, there are four of them, some might even say that attempting to align them is the ultimate game of Connect Four, connect them and you are officially winning at life.

I am of course talking about the remarkable quadruplet of people, food, travel and art.

'To have your health, even just sort of. To have friends, even only a few. To have hobbies or interests and the freedom to pursue them. To have spent this day free from some terrifying encounter with chaos is to be lucky. Just look around you and take a moment to feel how lucky you are. You get another day to live on this earth. Enjoy it'.

Sam Harris

Common People

Someone once told me that life is basically just a series of rooms and who we get stuck in those rooms with adds up to what our lives are. And I can't stop thinking about it.

Good people are out there. They exist. It's entirely possible to be in a relationship or a friendship free from shouting, abuse, ego, narcissism, judgement or negativity. A connection where mutual respect, open communication and genuine support create something truly magical.

'Surround yourself with people who fight for you in rooms you're not in'.

Unknown

I think it's worth saying it again: good people do exist. And they matter. In fact, we need them. They're everywhere, often appearing in our lives unexpectedly, and sometimes they're the ones we never thought we'd click with.

I wonder if anyone else out there has developed an odd mutual respect thing, going on with someone from school that you were never close to? It's pretty much all online but it's there, supportive and its real! I love it.

I'm incredibly grateful for the good people in my life. Some I see often, others rarely, and some – for various reasons – have left my life after many shared years and extraordinary moments. Yet, they all (nearly all) have one thing in common: they inspire me.

It's not just me they inspire; they have a knack for uplifting others too. Whether they're tackling social issues, contributing to education or creating art, they have a purpose that makes a difference in the world. They've dared to put themselves out there for what they're passionate about. They genuinely care about the world.

And they give a shit about me. They offer me genuine empathy. I'm in my 40s and I still need someone on occasion to tell me I'm okay. They make me feel understood and valued. And we laugh, a lot!

'Don't leave your coffee for too long and then be surprised why it's cold . . .

I'm not talking about coffee'.

@mik3y_says

Don't get me wrong, I've had my share of shitty people. Some who seemed great at first but revealed their true colours over time. Others gleaned all the learning and energy they could before jumping to their next energy source. And a few? Well, they morphed into full-blown bellends before my very eyes, and I can tell you nothing hurts more than your favourite person turning into a life lesson.

But this isn't about them. This is about the good ones, the ones who matter, who are worth finding, worth holding on to. Even the rare legends who have drifted away still leave their mark.

'There are some people who have sun inside them. It's hard to explain. Their presence just brightens, it's not about their beautiful smiles. They have an internal being that sheds light and feels like sun. It's a calm energy. Inner peace. But most importantly, it's not wanting anything back in return. It's sun'.

Anon

The thing about good people is that they are consistent. Whether at work, home, with others or on their own, they're the same person. They wear their heart on their sleeve and never shy away from how they're feeling. Good people don't judge, an absolute hallmark of a genuine person, they understand that everyone has their own path to walk and mistakes to make, and they respect that.

Good people hear you; they listen attentively. They check in. They find joy in the simple things, they notice glimmers, *your* glimmers. They're comfortable in their own skin when they're with you and they are always kind.

I recently, for the first time, heard the word 'Mattering'. Simply, Mattering is about how we treat ourselves and how we treat each other. Mattering captures the profound feeling that our actions, presence and contributions are meaningful and valued by others. I'd go as far to say that mattering is a fundamental human need. It's the warm glow of knowing you're valued, you matter, and this directly impacts upon our self-esteem and wellbeing.

This shit can't be faked. Well, it can, but only for so long, until it's found out.

'Your energy is your most expensive currency. And not everyone can afford it'.

Deja Rae

Guess Who?

The following is inspired by the philosophy of Charles Schulz, creator of the 'Peanuts' comic strip.

You don't have to actually answer the questions. Just ponder on them. Just read it straight through, and you'll get the point.

1. Name the five wealthiest people in the world.
2. Name the last five Olympic 100 metres winners.
3. Name the last five winners of Miss Universe.
4. Name 10 people who have won the Nobel or Pulitzer Prize.
5. Name the last half dozen Academy Award winners for best actor and actress.
6. Name the last decade's worth of Wimbledon winners.

'We all want to be famous people, and the moment we want to be something we are no longer free'.

Jiddu Krishnamurti

How did you do?

The point is, none of us remember all the headliners of yesterday. These are no second-rate achievers; they are the best in their fields.

But the applause dies. Awards tarnish. Achievements are forgotten. Accolades and certificates are buried with their owners.

'Strive not to be a success, but rather to be of value'.

Albert Einstein

Let's try another, see how you do with this one:

1. List a few teachers who aided your journey through school.

2. Name three friends who have helped you through a difficult time.

3. Name five people who have taught you something worthwhile.

4. Think of three people who have made you feel appreciated and special.

5. Think of five people you enjoy spending time with.

Easier? The lesson?

Popularity is not love. Likes on Instagram are not real. The people who make a difference in your life are not the ones with the most credentials, the most money or the most awards.

They are simply the ones who care the most.

'Make sure the important people in your life know how important they are before it's too late'.

Anon

I recall an article by Mark Manson from years ago, where he stated, *'A crisis doesn't change people; it amplifies who they already are'*. This notion has remained deeply ingrained in me, resonating particularly during times of crisis, be it my mental health, within family dynamics, professional circles or amidst a global crisis.

The world, I've come to believe, is teeming with remarkable individuals, I mean it, fucking remarkable. Whilst occasionally it may feel like they do, these individuals don't just appear out of thin air during difficult times; rather, they've always been among us.

Through all life throws at us, be it heartbreaks, breakdowns, health struggles, conflicts, or financial woes, these extraordinary souls are by our side. They inhabit our personal lives, professional lives, schools, supermarkets, hospitals, everywhere imaginable.

They were *already* great but when shit hits the fan, we see them, and more importantly, they see us. These moments give them a platform to shine. They don't ask for it, they don't do it for thanks, and most will never know how amazing, how supportive or how inspiring they are. Sometimes they save lives.

When we stop and think about it, one can't help but notice the multitude of people in our lives deserving of immense gratitude: family, friends, colleagues, caregivers, and clients. Whether it's their support, affection, encouragement, empathy, or mere presence, we often – unknowingly – take them for granted.

'Friends come and go like waves of the ocean, but the true ones stick like an octopus on your face'.

Anon

Recalling pivotal moments, such as navigating through the trials of COVID-19 or grappling with the fine print of being noticed, I've come to realise that these exceptional individuals were always present. It's not always the one's you expect. Again, it's during these trying times that our eyes are opened to their support, they see us, and in turn – to repeat myself – we see them.

We also see the ones who back off, the ones who disappear. Manson says, *'adversity seems to bring out not necessarily the worst in people, but the essence of people'.*

He's right, as I hit my lowest point ever, I learned quickly who knew me best, who noticed, who gave a fuck. Some I could have put money on being there, and while I will be forever grateful, some I really wasn't expecting to be, were!

And there were those I hoped would be there, but they weren't.

I remember someone once telling me. *'Only those who care about you, can hear you when you're quiet'.* And it's true, some didn't hear me.

Good people do things for other people.

That's it.

The end.

State of the Art

Imagine a world without art. No Frida Kahlo. No Bowie. No Freddie Mercury to lift our spirits and make us want to punch the air, no Julia Donaldson to transport us to new worlds or Banksy to capture the beauty and pain of life.

No Billy Connolly to make us laugh until we cry, no Moonwalk to bust on the kitchen floor or Rabbie Burns to set our hearts afire.

Art gives us a way to express emotions and ideas like nothing else. When we're overwhelmed by joy, grief or confusion, art becomes our voice, turning raw feelings into something tangible and beautiful. It's through this process that art becomes a beacon of hope, reminding us that even in our darkest moments, we can create something meaningful.

'Practice any art, music, singing, dancing, acting, drawing, painting, sculpting, poetry, fiction, essays, reportage, no matter how well or badly, not to get money and fame, but to experience becoming, to find out what's inside you, to make your soul grow'.

Kurt Vonnegut

But art does more than just reflect the world as it is, it dares to imagine the world as it could be. Every brushstroke, every note, every move, every word is a glimpse into an artist's vision of a better future. Art challenges us to see beyond our current circumstances, to envision new possibilities and to believe that change is possible. It's an act of defiance against despair, a bold statement that things can and will get better.

What's truly magical about art is its ability to connect us. Across cultures, languages and time, art speaks a universal language. It allows us to understand each other in ways that go beyond mere conversation. Through art, we realise that our struggles, hopes and dreams are shared. This connection fosters empathy and solidarity, filling us with hope that we're not alone on this journey.

I've always had a passion for writing, admired design, loved music and appreciated performance. As a kid, art to me was a picture on the wall, or something we did at school, I had no idea how broad 'art' is and how important it would become in my life. Or in the world for that matter. Art isn't just important, it's everything. It doesn't just sit on a wall or live in a book . . . it dances, it sings, it challenges and it celebrates everything that makes us gloriously human.

'Art is the highest form of hope'.

Gerhard Richter

Arts and culture help tackle social injustice, theatres, museums, comedy clubs, galleries and libraries are the beating heart of our towns and cities. Not only do they bring prosperity, but they also bring communities together and make life worth living.

It has a power over our hearts and our minds that can enchant, enlighten, amaze, confuse, comfort and astound us.

When I started writing comedy in my early teens, I hid it. I wasn't the funny kid, I wasn't the drama kid or the rock star kid. It was something I kept to myself, in my bedroom, behind a closed door. I hid me.

Here's to the next wave. Here's to the kids writing their lyrics. Here's to all the bands still to break through. To the painters who splash their souls across canvases, brushstrokes heavy with dreams.

To the dancers whose bodies move like fire, expressing what words can't touch. Here's to the poets scribbling on napkins, sharing their truth in verses that will one day change the world.

To the filmmakers who turn fleeting moments into stories that live forever. To the street artists colouring the concrete jungle, transforming the mundane into a masterpiece.

Future drag queens, prepare to slay . . . your spotlight is waiting!

Art isn't just a hobby, it's a force. It's rebellion. It's freedom. It's the heartbeat of our culture. It's how we protest, how we heal, how we connect when language fails. It reminds us that we're human. That we feel. That even in a world that can be cold and relentless, beauty exists, and we get to create it.

To the sculptors, the photographers, the video game designers, the graphic designers and the tattoo artists, your visions shape the world.

To the actors, the playwrights, the authors, the digital artists and every creator in between, you are the ones who remind us what it means to be alive.

Keep pushing, keep dreaming, keep making magic. Because art matters. It breathes life into the ordinary. It amplifies the unheard voices. It transcends time, breaks boundaries and changes lives.

Here's to artists, everywhere. You're creating the future, and we need your fire.

Take care of it, keep it burning.

Soul Food

I love sandwiches.

And I'm pretty sure you love sandwiches too. And if you don't, then you've never sandwiched properly. You're sandwiching wrong.

'If you want a healthy and happy life, you need to avoid dickheads. Not Carbohydrates'.

Michael Ulloa

In today's busy world, it's easy to forget to enjoy the simple things in life, like bread.

I love the bread. My goodness do I love the bread, it's like the most joyous of packaging. But it's the filling that counts, right? We can have the best bread but get the filling wrong and there are questions.

There's a fine line between too much and not enough. Mayo? Butter? Maybe both, maybe neither. Meat? Cheese? Both? Neither?

Salad? Salad cream?

Huge delicisiousions, sorry I'm salivating . . . decisions! To egg or not to egg?

Get it right, we're in sandwich heaven. Get it wrong, you'll know all about it.

'Gavin you're now just writing about sandwiches'.

Yes. Yes, I am.

As great leaders say, *'with great sandwiches comes great responsibility'.*

They're right, especially if you're the one making the sandwiches for everyone else. The pressure of sandwichship these days is huge.

All eyes are on you. Your entire legacy will be judged upon your sandwichship.

Don't quote me but I think it was Maya Angelou who said, *'Most people won't remember what you say or what you do, but they will remember how you made their sandwiches'*.

Sandwiches are life.

A bold statement, I know.

We're born, we live, we die. A life and death sandwich.

You see, the middle is the bit that's up for grabs. The filling is life itself. And truly living life to the full is not always guaranteed or definite. We all like different fillings but the most exciting part is you get to choose your own. Over time you begin to understand what you like, what works for you, what you want more of and what makes you want to puke. You get a little more daring and adventurous with your filling and sometimes all we want is 'just ham' or 'just cheese', which is fine if you want a dull sandwich. But if life's a sandwich – and you're the sandwich maker – why not fill it with epic ingredients?

'Remember, pain is just French for bread'.

Anon

If your sandwich is rubbish, or not exciting enough, or full of cucumber, why not start experimenting? Adjust the filling, try something new, discover new flavours, drop the bland, upgrade the ingredients.

It's hard though if you're leading the filling decisions for everyone, buffet style.

Sandwichship is of course not just about you. You're important but it's also about encouraging others to try something new, something different.

But you know and I know, not everyone likes onion.

Or houmous.

And they'll tell you.

Oh my god, will they tell you!

Even when you get it right, there won't be enough for everyone. Ever.

Sandwich conflict is real, and it can take its toll.

'Mayonnaise is just like lotion but for bread'.

Anon, 7 years old

Staying humble but remaining confident with our fillings is the key. Sometimes we need to accept that apple and cheese on a sandwich is weird. Weirdly *delicious*!

There's the fact that triangle sandwiches taste better. Crusts? No crusts?

And then there's the queen; the crisp sandwich.

Less regrets, more baguettes!

I'll stop there . . .

A good scran absolutely and utterly makes my heart sing. There's not much in the world that makes me happier than going out with family and friends for a great meal. It's amazing how flavour and texture can work their magic and create a remarkable shift in how we're feeling.

A simple – but great – cheeseburger (technically a sandwich) can brighten my day and send my spirits soaring. Cheeseburgers must be one of the greatest inventions of all time, right up there with penicillin, electricity, dishwashers and crisps.

Deliciousness is everywhere. It comes from our mother, our childhood, the room we are eating in, the country we happened to be visiting, the weather around us, the plates we are eating on and the friends we are eating with. It's mental as much as it is chemical.

When was the last time you really noticed what food does to you?

Food isn't just fuel, think about it, food can enhance your mood in seconds. One bite of something amazing, and suddenly you're transported, inspired, recharged. A handful of blueberries, a perfectly spiced chicken wing or a slice of cheese on an oatcake, each bite can be an adventure, an indulgence or even a revelation.

Can we all just take a moment to appreciate cheese . . .

Thank you, as you were.

Food is connection, it's present at every major life event, woven into every celebration, heartbreak, late-night talk and lazy Sunday mornings. Food is creativity in action, it's the art we taste, a canvas we can customise endlessly and our own personal 'reset' button when life gets overwhelming.

And let's not forget, food is magic. Plants turn sunlight into nourishment, and we transform it into strength, laughter and passion. Food makes us feel alive, makes us human and brings people together like nothing else can. Food is the gateway to emotions we didn't even know we had.

The right meal at the right time? Life-changing.

Move it or Lose it!

Travel should be considered an essential human activity. Many of us, me included, have taken travel for granted. From a walk through a neighbouring town to a journey across the world.

'Travel is not reward for working, it's education for living'.

Anthony Bourdain

Movement is wired into our DNA. Our ancestors didn't settle, they roamed across mountains and seas, driven by the promise of discovery. *'The great affair is to move'* as Robert Louis Stevenson so perfectly put it. It's not just about seeing new places; it's about feeling them in your bones. It's about that sudden realisation, you're more capable, curious and open than you thought.

You can't feel the vastness of the ocean or the silence of the woods through a screen, it's something you have to breathe in firsthand. Next time life feels too settled, remember, you're an adult, you can disappear into the woods anytime. You are, one might say, utterly outdoorable.

And while planes and road trips are great, don't underestimate the power of a simple walk. *'The longer the walk, the better the thoughts'* says Zach Pogrob. He's right, getting outside, even for a bit, reminds you of how big and weird and beautiful the world really is.

Movement is our default setting. So, embrace your inner nomad and skip, wander, run or just move. Because life's a journey, and as much as it holds a special place in my heart, the couch is no place for a soul on fire.

So, I'll ask again; is this all we are?

Is it fuck! We are so much more than society dictates.

What makes life great are the people we hold close, the ones who laugh with us until we're breathless, who stand by us when we feel lost. It's the meals shared, from humble picnics to feasts, where the food nourishes not just the body, but the heart. It's the late-night conversations where dreams and fears are laid bare in the company of those who understand you best. It's the moments that make us stop, breathe and feel alive, whether it's through art that moves us to tears or music that pulls us to our feet.

'Space is the breath of art'.

Frank Lloyd Wright

We are creators and dreamers, not collectors of things. We build meaning through what we give, what we share and how we move through the world, chasing beauty, joy and connection. It's not about the lavish, but the lived, the stories that unfold in the spaces between, the joy of dancing in your kitchen, of finding home in a place, a plate, or the eyes of someone we love.

Life isn't for amassing; it's for experiencing. For living fully, messily, beautifully and richly, in ways that no bank account can ever touch. So, we keep going, keep moving (skipping), keep laughing, because *that* is what makes life feel like it's bursting at the seams. Not what you have, but who you are, who you love and what you give.

And never forget, the body is our soul's only home, treat it wisely.

'Go to Glasgow at least once in your life and have a roll and square sliced sausage and a cup of tea. When you feel the tea coursing over your spice-singed tongue, you'll know what I mean when I say: It's good to be alive'.

Sir Billy Connolly

I'll say it again, we are so much more.

CHAPTER 5

Invisible Rucksack

*H*o'w do you fill yourself back up, Gavin?'

I stared at my feet for what felt like an eternity, trying desperately to answer the question. Eventually, I lifted my heavy head and looked up. I had nothing.

'*You deserve to be filled the same way you pour*'.

I felt that.

'*Where's your dad?*'

I still don't know why the doctor asked me this. She was brand new to the surgery, I'd never met her before, and she didn't know anything about me *or* him. There's no mention of my dad in my records, he's been dead for many years, and yet *this* was the question she thought to ask!

In this moment, something in my mind and body just gave. Maybe she just caught me off guard, but everything I was carrying came to the forefront and I broke, right there in the doctor's surgery. My invisible rucksack was turned inside out in record time. Years of me doing 'me things' to myself, emptied, gone and strewn all over the floor in a fucking mess, all unpacked in about 10 seconds flat.

Everything.

'All the clouds in me are raining'.

R.H. Sin

I cannot explain the hell I had been feeling in my head, but for the first time in a while, albeit with a tidal wave coming out my face, I felt a heaviness lifting.

Amidst the torrent of released emotions, this anti-hero had an epiphany: resilience apparently has a soft spot for vulnerability; asking for help, helps.

Who knew?!

In this moment my doctor picked up her pen and began to write. I couldn't see what she was putting down on paper, but I felt like I read her mind and knew exactly what she was thinking . . .

BINGO!

'Maybe the journey isn't so much about becoming anything. Maybe it's about un-becoming everything that isn't really you, so you can be who you were meant to be in the first place'.

Paulo Coelho

> **Mr Ping:** The secret ingredient is . . . *Nothing.*
>
> **Po:** . . . Huh?
>
> **Mr Ping:** You heard me, nothing. There *is* no secret ingredient!
>
> **Po:** Wait, wait. It's just plain old noodle soup? You don't add some kind of special sauce or something?
>
> **Mr Ping:** Don't have to. To make something special, you just have to believe it's special.

Too many people are searching for more than just tips and advice for life these days. So many crave a literal secret, the secret to a better life, a successful life, a happy life, whatever that even means nowadays!

We're all guilty of it.

What if there is no secret? What if that *is* the secret? What if the actual secret to actual life is that there is no actual secret?

It would blow the self-help/personal development industry to smithereens. All the 'Secret to a Happier Life' and 'How to be Successful' type books just instantly vanish!

I can see it now! A one-page book that blows all other books out the water!

The short conversation above between Mr Ping and his son Po is from the wonderful *Kung-Fu Panda*, a favourite movie of mine, crammed full of incredible life lessons!

Just like Po himself says to his arch nemesis, Tai Lung; ***it's okay, I didn't get it at first either***.

But *I* really didn't.

There is no secret ingredient. It's just you.

Not only is it just you, sometimes you get a little bit too attached to what you believe you are.

Guilty!

Po realises we don't need a secret ingredient. We don't need to be someone 'special'. We all have the potential already to be great.

Po embodies the essence of an anti-hero through his journey of self-discovery and unconventional approach to heroism. Initially, he appears as a bumbling and overweight panda with no traditional martial arts skills, defying the archetype of a typical hero. His journey is riddled with self-doubt, as he struggles to fit into the rigid expectations of the Kung Fu world.

Familiar! Well, minus the Kung Fu part, obvs.

Po identifies with 'me' as fat, lazy and not really capable of doing great things. But he doesn't want to be 'me' anymore, he wants to change.

Familiar!

Sitting in the doctor's surgery that day, I didn't want to be me anymore. What I had been through had burst open the floodgates of what felt like hell. It brought difficult memories and feelings to the forefront of my mind. I had shit to deal with and even with no energy left and an empty rucksack, I wanted change. I needed change.

'Your idea of me is not my responsibility to live up to'.

Anon

What sets Po apart is his resilience and unwavering determination to overcome his limitations, embracing his uniqueness and using it to his advantage.

Po's unorthodox methods often challenge the norms and traditions of the Kung Fu world, making him a symbol of rebellion against the established order.

Despite his flaws and occasional missteps, Po ultimately proves himself as a hero through acts of bravery, loyalty and selflessness. His journey is one of growth and redemption, as he learns to harness his inner strength and embrace his true identity.

In the movie, a soothsayer foretold the destiny of the villainous Lord Shen, that 'a warrior of black and white' will stand against him and defeat him. Shen deduces that the warrior will be a panda, therefore raids all of the Gongmen city with his wolf army and attempts to exterminate all the pandas. Some of them fled and many got killed.

During this time Po's mom hides him in a basket of radishes which were to be delivered to Mr Ping, the goose who later adopts him.

Years later destiny finds both of them face to face. Po defeats Lord Shen and his entire army. Po comes to him in the midst of the ruins, Shen is breathing heavily . . .

Shen: How did you find peace? I took away your parents. Everything. I scarred you for life.

Po: See. That's the thing Shen. Scars heal.

Shen: No, they don't. Wounds heal.

Po: Oh yeah. So, what do scars do? They fade I guess.

Shen: I don't care what scars do.

Po You should, Shen. You gotta let go of the stuff you carry in the past cause it just doesn't matter. The only thing that matters is: What you choose to be now.

'Choosing yourself can be a struggle especially if you've been conditioned to choose others from the time you were younger, but it's never too late to start now. It's never too late to prioritise yourself, even if tending to you seems unfamiliar and foreign at first'.

Billy Chapata

Choosing 'me' is tough because 'me' is not the average option. 'Me' is the wild card, the dreamer, the giver, the peacemaker, the relentless pursuer of what matters. Picking 'me' means you're ready for an adventure, willing to step into the unknown and eager to shine. It's a leap into the extraordinary, a chance to leave mediocrity behind, to learn and to grow.

I came across this quote recently and once again, I can't stop thinking about it . . .

'Accidentally spent all my life making sure everyone else around me feels comfortable, only to realise I never felt comfortable the whole time'.

And that my friends hits really fucking hard.

Watch You Don't 'Should' Yourself

Ever had a bad dose of the 'shoulds'? Awful, isn't it?

The 'shoulds' have an uncontrollable nature about them. There's literally never a good time, they're uncomfortable, often arriving without warning.

On occasion, no matter what you do, 'shoulds' just keeps coming, whether you want them or not! Sometimes it's like someone turned on a tap, a never-ending, excessive release of 'should' which can overflow and overwhelm our entire being.

'But those Woulda-Coulda-Shouldas all ran away and hid from one little Did'.

Shel Silverstein

The 'shoulds' are often accompanied by a very uncomfortable sensation. A heaviness. Sometimes physical but there is almost always emotional discomfort as the intense pressure builds. Draining *and* distressing, it can get messy, especially if you 'should' yourself in public.

There's nothing worse than being caught short! We've all been there, the impact this can have on our mental and emotional wellbeing is huge.

It's really hard to concentrate and make good decisions when you have the 'shoulds', they're highly disruptive and can ruin even the best of days.

With every bout of 'shoulds' the burden is huge, always accompanied by an incredible desire for relief. Relief from pressures you never thought your body could produce.

Bruce Lee spoke about Shouldism, something he described in his private letters as *'growing up completely surrounded by what you should and should not do, spending much of your time playing a game with yourself'*, a game he called the 'Self-improvement Game' or the 'Self-torture Game'.

Shouldism is based on the phenomenon of dissatisfaction. It's a clever wee thinking style that creeps into our mind leading to all sorts of anxiety and sadness. The sneaky wee fucker becomes automatic, lurking in the shadows of our daily lives and my shadow was like a black bear that followed me everywhere.

Society dictates, demands and expects so much of humans from such a young age. And rarely does anyone teach you that it's ok to ignore most of it. Whether we like it or not, *everyone* is influenced by society. While cultural and societal expectations can differ depending on age and location, they exist, everywhere!

'Don't let "should" rob you of the joy of what "could" be'.

Anon

I think we can all agree that, since birth, we're force-fed ideas of who we should be and what we should believe, and failure to meet these societal expectations may leave you feeling like you're not successful enough or good enough for those around you.

I talk a lot of should.

I am highly skilled in taking all that disapproval from others, soaking it up like a sponge and then turning it against myself.

As humans, our inner critics, that sound suspiciously like the voices of our parents, teachers and society, all mix together in one toxic blend, kicking our asses!

And the guilt that comes with it, well, that weighs heavy on the soul.

I think it's important to note that we *all* get to decide which societal expectations we are happy to align with. Or to put it slightly differently, *you* get to choose which societal expectations align with *your* core values?

Ask yourself this; Have you ever come across anyone who's become the best version of themselves by following societal norms and expectations?

Didn't think so. In many cases, quite the opposite . . .

Your idea of happiness won't be the same as mine. Good, I guess, but we need to educate young people that it's ok to focus on their own idea of what it means to be happy and successful, to forge their own path and to distance themselves from the comfort of the herd and follow their calling, without caring much about what others think of them.

Maybe it's not just the young ones that need to hear it. It's hard, I'm in my 40s and I still carry a lifetime of 'shoulds' in my invisible rucksack.

By the time I finally went to the doctor, I think I was overdosing on 'shoulds'. It was heavy.

The worst part is I often don't even realise it's happening. Sometimes I can't stop 'shoulding' myself and yeah, sometimes I should myself in public. I recently should myself on stage, playing by the rules that I have swallowed whole, without ever stopping to question them.

'The "shoulds" in life are like weeds in a garden; they choke out the beauty of possibility'.

Unknown

Aye, the 'shoulds'. They've haunted us all, haven't they? A relentless wee chorus in the back of the mind, droning away like a fucking bagpipe that's out of tune. Sorry to inform you, even though some other books will tell you there is, there is *no* tidy wee checklist for life.

When we give in to the 'shoulds' we often start living lives that aren't ours, chasing goals that don't resonate with our true selves.

There's so many 'shoulds' that have haunted me for years. I should have life all figured out. I should have made it by now. I should be more successful. I should hide my anxiety. I should just make sure others are happy. I should be skinnier.

Maybe we all need to do some 'we *shouldn't* be doing this' things.

Make a Noise They Said

In 2002, at the age of 23, I travelled to Australia to perform for a month at the Melbourne International Comedy Festival. Very little performing experience, other side of the world, no money, no following, didn't know another soul.

People were taken aback, shocked even, at the news of me going. It's just not the done thing!

But I did it.

My point? I can't *believe* I did it.

It broke all the rules of what society dictated to me as the norm. I'm not sure I could do it now. Actually, scrap that, I *couldn't* do it now. It just feels like such a weight, I can feel my anxiety building just at the thought of it.

I left my small town on the west coast of Scotland, on this occasion with a rucksack packed full of hopes, dreams and ideas, arrived in Australia and unpacked the whole thing as fast I as could.

At our first official comedy festival meeting, they made me feel so welcome but were quick to remind me that I was a nobody, and I had a shitload of tickets to sell.

Fine. I had no fear. I thought to myself, 'I'll just sell them'.

They told me of a huge media gathering that takes place each year in Melbourne City Square, a chance for every single act to be seen, to be heard and to promote their show. This was pre-social media. *Everyone* was going to be there.

'Make a noise', they said.

'I'll book a pipe band', that was my first thought, obvs.

So I did.

'The bravest thing you can do is show the world who you truly are'.

Anon

And when I came around that corner, bagpipes blasting, every single camera turned.

I chose 'me', and I was ready to shine, full fucking beam.

And I did, for years.

And then the light went out.

Who Put the Big Light Off?

Throughout my 20s and early 30s my days were filled with wonder and fascination. Every day I was five again, exploring, dreaming, playing, writing, performing.

Think about how wee kids face the world, with curiosity and an open heart. I was driven by nothing but sheer enjoyment and exploration, it just felt so natural and fun.

And then it didn't.

'I am out with lanterns looking for myself'.

Emily Dickinson

It all started when I lost my dad. My dad was a big light in my life, but I never appreciated how big. And when that light went out, my world got a little darker and I got a little quieter.

I thought I had dealt with it like a pro. I hoped I had done all the right things.

But death brings change. Death shifts our focus. Death introduces new pressures. Death tests our resilience.

Death means grief. Grief means loss. Loss means change.

And it's exhausting.

All Good Things Must Come to an End

They say all good things must come to an end. You, me, everyone and everything. Except every plastic toy from the 1980s and 1990s, and LEGO, obviously. It's made of plastic and will literally be here forever.

I actually love LEGO. It's remarkable the hours that can go into it. I must have clocked up months of playing with the stuff. It's a huge investment. Yes, financially but more so time, energy and effort. It's very similar to life.

Think about it. For all the joy and fun LEGO can bring us, it can bring pain and anguish too. In fact, there's only one thing more painful than stepping on LEGO and that's *kneeling* on LEGO! Fact! But it's true, life can be painful too.

'LEGO', in Danish, actually means 'play well' and as we all know, life is best lived when it's played well.

LEGO sometimes comes in a massive box of random bits. You tip them out onto the carpet and start creating something amazing. LIFE's also like that, you have to piece the bits together to create something amazing, weird or random. LEGO is about building. LIFE is about building (friendships, knowledge, skills, interests, abilities, experience . . . *ourselves*).

But sometimes LEGO isn't random. It comes in a kit. You open it up and the bits are grouped in little bags with numbers on them. There's a picture and a plan. It's quite complicated, it takes a while, and you might need someone to help, but if you stick with it, you will end up with something that looks a bit like the picture on the box. For some people, life can be like that. They have an idea in their mind about what they want to achieve – a goal, a dream, an ambition – and if they stick to it and follow the instructions, they'll achieve it in the end. Or something that looks a bit like it. Plus, life is always easier when we reach out for help with the tricky bits.

Life is a gift. It was given to you by your parents. If you haven't thanked them for it, and you still can, please do. Quite often, LEGO is also a gift. More likely a birthday prezzie from your Auntie Susan. She needs thanking too.

And if you think LEGO has some random characters, it's got nothing on the real-life characters we meet along the way.

'If you can't handle me randomly blurting out song lyrics that relate to what you just said, we can't be friends'.

Anon

Thinking Minds

It's okay to start over. Sometimes, you get it right; sometimes you don't. With LEGO *and* life, the aim is to learn from your attempts, mistakes and failures, and *keep on building*.

LEGO can be messy. As can life. Sometimes it's all about the tidy up. A clear out. Repackaging can be healthy. And then passing it on to someone else feels great.

The truth is, we're all just kind of making it up. It's a huge secret that most people don't tell you. No one really 100% knows what they're doing 100% of the time.

I'm old enough to remember the days when LEGO used to claim that a free dinosaur came with every pack, sometimes a free aeroplane. Very clever marketing when you think about it!

You'll likely remember *Forest Gump* starring Tom Hanks, his memorable line was *'Mama says life is like a box of chocolates, you never know what you're gonna get'*.

I reckon life is more like an enormous box of LEGO. But with it comes a free YOU. Better than any dinosaur or aeroplane. And you can build your free YOU any way, shape or size you want. You can add pieces, change parts, start over, you can sometime lose a wee piece of you, that's also ok and we learn a million lessons along the way.

But remember, there are billions of pieces. Life is often complicated, as hard as we try to manage all the pieces, life – or Lego for that matter – is rarely simple. But when we stick at it, try new things, have the courage to fail and start again, when it works it's a magical thing.

And just like in life, there are always easier routes and safer options. There's always DUPLO. It's not nearly as exciting and you definitely won't get it stuck up your nose!

Very few of us have a full Lego set still fully built and in one piece. Like life, a piece will fall out from time to time, or we lose a key piece that holds everything (or in my case, everyone) together.

Little Deaths

We actually experience loss a lot more than we realise.

We experience what Frank Ostaseski calls 'little deaths' almost daily. We might lose a piece of jewellery, a key, a shoe, money, anything really.

But you know and I know, it's not just 'little deaths', unfortunately loss comes in all shapes and sizes.

It can be job shaped, energy shaped, relationship shaped, confidence shaped, sleep shaped, freedom shaped, independence shaped, dream shaped, pet shaped . . . everything shaped.

Even phone shaped.

Phone shaped?

Yeah.

Imagine the scenario . . .

It's a Friday evening and you're 16 years old. You're thinking about heading out to meet some friends but you're running a little late. You know there's a party happening, you're just about to find out where and boom . . .

Your phone freezes . . . and then it switches off. It won't come back on. It flickers . . . and dies.

Your phone is dead.

We don't need to be 16 to know how this feels, it's not just a spanner in the works, this is an entire bag of spanners in life. It sucks and it's often followed by what I'm calling 'the 5 stages of phone death'. And as we're 16 and down with the kids, we're going to turn to the Urban Dictionary to explain the journey we go on with this:

1. **_WTAF?_** – Your first reaction is of horror and disbelief. You cannot believe this happening to you when you are already running late. You try to start the phone again and again and again. Charger is in, you're holding down buttons for 15 seconds. You know the drill. Aaargh!

2. **_Raging_** – Now that you realise the phone cannot be switched on, you can feel your blood boiling. _All_ the swear words fly through your head. It's clearly your parents' fault as they bought you the phone in the first place. Your friends are probably trying to call you. You're going to miss the party . . . FOMO is kicking off, right?

3. **_Hostage Situation_** – Even though you know it won't help, and it's a little weird, you start talking to your phone like it's a hostage situation! It's negotiation time. You're asking it nicely to start, just once. You tell it you'll keep it maintained, get the battery charged as soon as possible and love it forever. You're making promises that you know you can't keep as you pat it gently.

4. **_Totes Pressed_** – You basically turn into Eeyore. All the negative thoughts start rushing to your mind. You begin to feel depressed, sad and hopeless. You see no way out of the situation. Your life is ruined. It's over. Just what will people say? You could cry. It's the end of the world.

5. *Frustreptance* – Levels of frustration are high but you're beginning to accept the situation. After a firm talking to from your own self, you figure out what you should do next. Your mum has your mate's mum's number. Easy, you just call her, explain what's happened, she gives you the details and texts your mate to let them know you're going to be late. Sorted.

Or, worse case, you can't get your phone working, your mum doesn't have your mate's mum's number, you have no other way of communicating so you can't go to the party. Tough! You take it on the chin, and you get over it. You'll live. Life goes on.

Some of you will recognise this as the '5 stages of grief' which of course is the exact same as the '5 stages of change'. Shock & Denial – Anger – Bargaining – Depression – Acceptance.

It's the Kubler-Ross change curve of course. The emotional rollercoaster. I'm not sure if you know this . . . you've been on it for years. Since about 2020 we've basically seen something akin to the Kubler-Ross curve play out across the world, it just doesn't seem to want to end.

But if we look closely, we've seen the machinery of humanity working, overcoming crises and moving on. As evolution will tell you, change is mostly progressive, with slow advancement over time. But occasionally, it's accelerated by cataclysmic events. COVID-19 was/is the perfect example. And even now, as a result, some of us are knackered.

Some of us are not ok.

It's important to note that the five stages of grief/change are not always experienced in the same order. Some fly through them, others bounce around between them for some time. I've been through them all over the last few years. To the mix I can add shock, loneliness, sadness, guilt and extreme anxiety.

It's hugely overwhelming and confusing at the time. It doesn't feel normal, but it is.

We can learn a lot from loss. Remember the list form earlier, it can be job shaped, energy shaped, relationship shaped, confidence shaped, freedom shaped, dream shaped, pet shaped, sleep shaped, everything shaped, phone shaped.

But they do say, from endings come new beginnings. Even the big losses, the human shaped ones that leave us feeling lost and struggling to find our way.

For Flux Sake

There is so much change in the world today, it's coming thick, it's coming fast and it's relentless. Sometimes we need to slow down and truly see what's happening around us. Imagine you could flip your perspective, re-evaluate how you see and, in turn, how you show up every day.

We all know change is complicated and messy. Yet it also defines today, tomorrow and beyond. So, let's think of this as leaning into . . . let's call it 'certain uncertainty'.

'If the path before you is clear, you're probably on someone else's'.

Carl Jung

To lean into change calls for a shift in mindset, a way of thinking that recognises constant change and uncertainty as inherent features of life, not as flaws to be fixed. It's about reshaping your relationship with change from the inside out.

Imagine viewing every change – whether big or small, whether you want it, anticipate it, or not – as a wonderful opportunity rather than a looming threat. Imagine having the ability to see the silver linings in situations, to spot the glimmers that change gifts to us, all around, harnessing them to propel yourself forward with the energy and inspiration I spoke of in chapter one from those joyous sunkick moments.

This mindset shift changes change! It changes it from a perceived pain in the arse, into a powerful best pal. By welcoming change, you open the door to growth, learning and endless possibilities. By leaning into change, you embrace the adventure and unlock the potential within every twist and turn of your journey.

Whilst it isn't easy, and doesn't always feel like it, there are always glimmers and silver linings waiting to be harnessed.

But, the only way to truly embrace change is to dive headfirst into it. The big goal is not to lose you, but to get beautifully, wonderfully lost in the experience of change. That's where the magic happens. Getting lost is often how we find our way.

Starter. Main. Starter.

Yeah, you read that right.

Starter. Main. Then . . . another starter.

This is something my brother and I have done for years. He started it. It blew my mind the first time he did it. It felt so wrong, so illegal and yet just so 'why the hell have I never done this?'

Why is it so weird?

Recently, a chef left his kitchen to come and shake my hand, called me a legend and went back to work. Why? Because I ordered scallops for pudding.

Not to be awkward. Not to cause a scene. I just don't always want dessert. Sometimes I want to finish with something not sweet. Something different. Something I want.

And here's the thing, I'm allowed. We're all allowed.

We're taught to follow a certain order. We're raised in a world of courses. Not just on menus. In life. There's a 'proper' order. An accepted rhythm.

Go to school, pick a path, uni, get a job, climb the ladder, and if you're good and don't rock the boat too much, you get dessert; retirement, pension, a nice view from the care home . . .

But what if the bit you're supposed to wait for . . . isn't the bit you actually want?

What if you don't want dessert at all?

What if, halfway through the 'main course' of your career, you suddenly think, 'This isn't for me', and fancy going back for more of the stuff that made you feel alive when you were 23 and a little bit unhinged?

It's not illegal, you know.

We act like it is, like changing direction is some form of betrayal. Like we've signed a contract with life that says, 'Must stick to path. Must be sensible. Must eat pannacotta, even though it's basically sad milk'.

(for the record, I LOVE pannacotta)

Here's a radical idea: you can reorder your life. No one's going to arrest you for doing what actually feels good.

Want to start over? Go for it.

Want to try something completely different and potentially fail spectacularly? Absolutely.

Because the truth is, a lot of people are full, but not satisfied. Full to the brim with the 'right' choices. Ticking all the boxes. Hitting all the milestones. Looking successful, sounding successful . . . but quietly bored out of their minds.

So maybe, instead of forcing ourselves to follow the script, we give ourselves permission to freestyle a bit. Go back for seconds of what we *actually* love. Even if it's messy. Even if it doesn't make sense on paper. Even if it means getting lost. Even if it means answering the dreaded question: 'So what are you doing these days?' with 'Honestly, I've got no idea, but I'm weirdly happy'.

There's power in that.

There's magic in saying: 'This thing? It used to work. It doesn't anymore. I'm changing it'.

It's not flaky. It's honest. It's brave. It's living on purpose instead of autopilot.

So go on, ask for another starter.

Change careers. Move cities. Unlearn half the stuff you thought was mandatory. Get weird with it. Get playful. Try something that might not work, and then do it again with better snacks.

You don't need permission.

Just appetite.

Emotionally Off-Roading

Big news; your relationship with change can improve. Mine too. It starts with understanding the types of change that piss you off and why they do so.

Think about it, getting lost in the wild landscape of change isn't a disaster. It's an adventure. Sure, we're often taught from a young age that getting lost is some sort of failure, a sign we've made a mistake. But guess what? That's the old script talking. In this weird world where change is the only constant, getting lost is the new normal!

Many of us at times feel completely disoriented, like our compass has gone haywire. The thing to remember is we don't get to choose this ever-changing planet we live on.

'No rebellious heart is ever at ease with paths established by others'.

B.W. Powe

Once you flip the script and embrace a sunkick mindset, getting lost becomes your superpower. It's not about wandering aimlessly; it's about stepping out of your comfort zone and seeking out the unknown. Getting lost doesn't mean you're clueless, it means you're brave enough to explore.

Remember, it's all about your response. Does getting lost make you anxious or curious? Do you freeze up or embrace the journey?

I've been there. Whether it's losing a loved one, starting a business, losing a business, a pandemic, navigating new relationships, being ghosted by best friends, switching careers, battling mental health challenges, losing hope or losing all meaning.

Life can be seriously shit.

But then, during the pandemic, whether we wanted it or not, the world delivered the slowdown I mentioned earlier, and we had a choice. I discovered that getting lost is a gift. The old script was shattered. More change means more getting lost.

Now, with the world doing what it's doing, feeling the way it's feeling, it's time to get lost in the best of ways: finding comfort in discomfort, seeing the familiar in the unfamiliar, and uncovering what you've been searching for all along.

Sure, we've all heard it: 'the journey shapes the destination'. What if the thrill, the true adventure, lies in the unknown? You might have a diary packed with appointments and Google Maps guiding your every step. Maybe you have someone keeping you on track. I have all of that, and I love my job, but it's stressful and it makes me anxious.

Without these things . . . well, actually, without these things, I'm on holiday. But without these things I'm lost. And I learned during COVID, that sometimes, I *can* like it.

I had my eyes opened, uncertainty brings excitement, if you want it to. It sparks creativity, new ideas and a fresh perspective, if you let it. I learned that if you lift your head and pay attention, truly notice what's around you, it can change your life.

'You are under no obligation to remain the same person you were a year ago, a month ago, or even a day ago. You are here to create yourself, continuously'.

Richard Feynman

I mentioned being on holiday. I love to go to new places and get lost. Just wandering . . . and wondering. The spontaneity, the being in the moment, the . . . just going with it. Cut off from the norm, the routine.

I also mentioned earlier that we're taught from a young age to *not* get lost. But when we do, we find our way. We ask for directions, seek help and gain guidance. We experience a slice of life we'd otherwise miss. Adventure and getting lost go hand in hand. It leads to surprises, self-discovery, new landscapes, glimmers and bursts of creativity.

Getting lost might make you feel like an outsider, but it also offers new perspectives and ideas. It's a crucial part of discovering what's truly important to you. Our brains love problem-solving, and getting lost fine-tunes our awareness of our surroundings.

When we're too comfortable, we miss what's right in front of us. We don't see the ordinary magic that is all around us. Our glimmers go unnoticed.

You're reading this book right now, or perhaps listening on download, but did you know that getting lost in a book reduces stress, sharpens the mind, improves sleep and fosters a sense of belonging? In other words, when we connect to something bigger than us, a story, a purpose, it encourages us to think, feel and re-imagine the type of person we want to be. Similarly, getting lost in your life or your work boosts resilience.

If you are feeling lost, dare to wander, let your curiosity guide you. Easier said than done – trust me, I know – but try not to fear it. See it as an invitation to explore, to grow and to rediscover the wonder that exists in every twist and turn.

Remember it's okay to walk away from things that make you unhappy. After all, it's often in our moments of uncertainty that we find the most profound clarity and the truest versions of ourselves.

Just keep in mind, you can't walk away from yourself.

Gav's 'When You Feel Like Shit' Checklist

If you're having a tough day, try one of these:

1. **Drink ice-cold water like it's a shot of hope** – Dance while doing it.

2. **Step outside for five minutes** – No phone. No filters. Just you, air and the universe quietly rooting for you. You are free to run as fast as you can . . . because you can. Skip.

3. **Write down the absolute shittest thought in your head** – Then respond like you're your most loyal, hilarious best mate. (Be the friend you need.)

4. **Ask yourself: 'What would Elmo do?'** – The answer is always 'hug it out and laugh from the belly'.

5. **Watch a video of a goat eating Doritos** – Trust the process.

6. **Hug someone or something** – Human, dog, cat, pillow, tree, alpaca, warm laundry.

7. **Whisper this: 'I'm doing my fucking best'** – Then say it again. Louder. Like you mean it. Because you do. Sing it full 'West End' if you need to!

8. **Put on 'that tune', you know the one, and go full dancefloor in your kitchen** – Air guitar *and* full air drumkit.

9. **Find one glimmer** – A decent cup of tea. A funny cloud. Smell a baby. Count it. Let it count.

10. **Declare a Temporary Life Timeout** – Go fetal burrito in a blanket, guilt-free. You are *not* a productivity machine. Ice cream.

CHAPTER **6**

Does Anyone Know What to Do?

But seriously, *does* anyone know what to do? Like, in general.

Does anyone actually know *how* to life? I mean, what – from the bottom of my heart – the fuck is going on in the world? Is this all because I didn't forward that email to 10 people in 2005?

Fuctifano ['fuktifano]

A Scottish phrase, meaning 'fuck'd if I know'. Normally used as a response to a question you do not know the answer to.

I have an intriguing notion to share with you; we're all just making it up, right?

Life, I mean.

No one' got it sussed, right?

Right?

Have you ever paused amidst the busyness to ponder the sheer, bewildering spectacle of it all?

'Years from now, all that will be left of you will be a lingering smile you left in the street once upon a time from a moment of unexplained happiness. A happiness that arrived without a plan, a beautiful glitch in the system. And someone's gonna stroll right through the space where you planted that smile and feel good for seemingly no reason at all'.

Darby Hudson

We're so busy doing all sorts of shit, all the time, that I often wonder if it's worth the stress and the anxiety when everything is going to disappear.

All of it.

Literally.

Think about it; you, your family, your friends, your job, your pets, your car, your clothes, your house . . . everything is going to disappear.

100 years from now, no one will know who you were. Someone else will live in your house. All your stuff will be gone.

Did you notice how fast last week went? The last 10 years?

So, is it worth it?

What if everything we do is essentially for nothing?

Bear with me, how often do you truly accept that all those late nights, all that hustle, might not actually amount to anything?

So, here's a biggie; is it possible that knowing you are mortal is actually your greatest power?

No one wants you to *actually* know that it's all for nothing because if everyone knew life wasn't just about the grind, the whole system would come crashing down. And that's exactly why this is such a big thought.

According to Therapist, Matthew Jones, once you get that everything you build – your career, your business, your relationships, your materialistic collection of shite – will eventually fade away, you gain a magical perspective on everything that happens in your life.

Every failure? It's just another chance to learn. Every success? A lesson in letting go. Every moment? A reason to celebrate and appreciate.

Facing this reality gives you the power to live a life that truly matters.

It makes you treasure every tiny detail of your day: the way the grass moves in the wind, a sea of ice-lolliness, the absurdity of rush-hour traffic. Everything shines brighter when you realise how precious and fleeting it all is.

'The future is a concept, it doesn't exist. There is no such thing as tomorrow. There never will be, because time is always now. That's one of the things we discover when we stop talking to ourselves and stop thinking. We find there is only present, only an eternal now'.

Alan Watts

Not so Fun Fact: we are all going to die.

Fun fact: at your funeral the only thing anyone will care about is what kind of human you were and each of us will be remembered in one of two ways, one of the good guys, or an arsehole.

Truth time: the essence of life lies in the moments we fully embrace and in always doing the right thing. And – in the words of Fat Boy Slim – the one time we can truly do both these things is . . .

Right here, right now.

Goals Really Do Come True

Goal setting . . . I know, YAWNFEST! But trust me, this technique is absolutely not about the future, this is about right here, right now.

But before we get to it, let's talk about laughing at inappropriate times.

Have you ever laughed so hard it hurts? Isn't it just wonderful? Have you ever laughed so hysterically you can barely speak, there's tears, snot, pee and you've forgotten how to breathe?

Again, wonderful . . . kinda!

'I don't trust anyone who doesn't laugh'.

Maya Angelou

But have you ever done it at a time you shouldn't? Isn't it just awful? You can't stop. You don't even know why you're laughing, and you're trying so hard not to, but it's happening anyway.

We've all got that friend or colleague who makes it even worse if they're in the room. You just know not to look at them or you're a goner. But you can't help yourself, can you? You catch their eye and that's it, game over!

School, college, university, work, anywhere. Hilarious *yet* horrendous! If there was ever a time we'd gladly let time speed up until we're out the other side, this is it.

Funerals are the worst. Funny stories are often shared but it's that weird uncomfortable feeling of 'am I meant to laugh at this?' that makes us laugh more than normal. It's a funeral, every bone in our body tells us we shouldn't be laughing. This is a sad, sombre occasion. But once you start, sometimes there's just no stopping.

I often think that this makes it harder sometimes. The tone of the event, or the environment we happen to be in, can often dictate a seriousness in the room. We just know don't we, it's not a time for laughter. It's a time for manners, respect and sensibleness.

And this just makes it worse . . .

A few years ago, I was at an awards night. A proper fancy type of affair with canapes, bubbly and bowties. I don't own a bowtie, I had to opt for the second-class regular tie. In the room were some of the most successful people in the world. A who's who of the business community. It felt very professional, very serious and extremely grown up.

I felt very nervous, very out of place and to add to this, I was up for an award. This was a big deal to me and there were huge cash prizes up for grabs for those with the best business ideas.

Like all award nights, there was a special guest, and this particular guest had been the successful recipient of the top prize from the previous year. He was awarded a six-figure sum that had transformed his business and, rightly so, he was there to share his incredible journey of how the prize money was used to develop a brand new and extraordinary piece of technology that will revolutionise the world of engineering.

I'm not going to lie, I barely understood a word he said. A cracking guy with a cracking business but it was all flying *way* over the top of my head. Hundreds of people around the room appeared to be hanging off every word he said. I'm sure it was all hugely impressive but with my non-existent attention span, the words he was saying were all blurring into one great big technology themed, intellectually-too-much-for-me presentation that left me feeling even more out my depth.

And then something unbelievably silly happened.

He said the words, *'Reverse pumping'*.

Well . . .

Everything went into slow motion.

I didn't know where to look so I looked down at my feet.

Then he said it again, *'Reverse pumping'*.

And again.

I don't care how childish this sounds. I know this is stupid, I understand he had a context. But at this moment, this was the funniest thing I had ever heard.

He kept saying it, *'Reverse pumping'*.

All I could think was *'stop saying it, please stop saying it'*.

In huge, big colourful letters it appeared on the screen. Each letter about a metre tall, REVERSE PUMPING.

My entire body was going into some kind of pre-laughter spasm. I was visibly shaking; I could barely breathe.

'I love people who make me laugh. I honestly think it's the thing I like most, to laugh. It cures a multitude of ills. It's probably the most important thing in a person'.

Audrey Hepburn

All I heard next was *'Teaching others to reverse pump'*. Again, I was aware of other words being said but it was like my brain was deliberately shutting them out, once again ignoring the context.

'The benefits of reverse pumping' came next, and it was here I made a schoolboy error.

I turned and I looked at my business partner and yes, eye contact was made.

I was gone.

Have you ever tried to laugh uncontrollably in silence? Of course you can't, it's uncontrollable.

This is the very type of laughter that earns you looks of absolute disgust, the type of laughter that ensures you're never invited back again. People were pointing. I had to leave and go for some fresh air.

Looking back on it, it's still funny but it's not *that* funny. It was just one of those moments that catches you unexpectedly and snowballs beyond belief. I actually met the guy later that evening and congratulated him on his success. He was genuinely fascinating and taught me that sometimes by reversing things, we gain a different perspective therefore we find solutions and achieve results we might never have experienced had we followed traditional methods.

And believe it or not, I had a bit of a moment on the way home, his words stuck with me. Not the pumping part, the reverse part, and this leads me to the next part of this book, and just a heads up, it's a biggie . . .

Goal setting. *Reverse* goal setting to be exact. Not nearly as funny as reverse pumping but this will change your life, now.

You Don't Have to Wait for Anything

As you'll read in the next chapter, I'm a big fan of allowing yourself to dream. But dreams don't come true without getting off your backside and making them happen.

You could say dreams are the easy part. And they're free too! But remember, they're imaginary, so we need the goals to make the wonderful visions in your head become real. It's the goals that get us results.

Dreams are mega important, they inspire us, but it's the goals that bring the focus to change our lives.

Goal setting is massive. In fact, it's an industry. Google alone lists over 20 million results for 'goal setting'. There are books dedicated to this stuff. Planners, worksheets, coaches, articles, businesses and residential experiences aimed at perfecting our technique. In turn, there are millions upon millions of us trying to achieve them.

One of the biggest problems with goal setting is that most people fail. They have a cost: time, money, effort, sweat, tears and sometimes your family/friends. If we were successful, we'd all be healthy, wealthy, happy and fulfilled. Our yachts would line the streets because our waterways would be full of our other yachts.

We are forever asked questions such as: Where do you see yourself in five years? What do you want to have achieved in life by the time you retire? It's all very future-focused.

The challenge with 'where do you see yourself' type questions is that the 'you' 5–10 years from now will be a very different 'you' to right now.

It never ends. 1 year from now, 5, 10, 20 years and on it goes. We just keep moving the goalposts, climbing more ladders, striving, aiming, looking ahead, working for the future.

'I think everyone should get rich and famous and do everything they ever dreamed of so they can see that it's not the answer'.

Jim Carrey

It's hard to guess what will make us happy in 10 years. Worry less about the future, it's got you covered, it's got its eye on you. I'm willing to bet though; you know what would make you happy right now.

At 13 years of age, we're asked to think about our career choices and choose school subjects that will put us on the right path. I can recall being asked in high school 'Where do you see yourself in 20 years?'. Really? I'm 13 mate, I'm just worried about how to get rid of my moobs and talk to girls!

Traditional goal setting is all about the future. Set a huge goal and break it down into manageable chunks. Start at the beginning and then lay it all out step by step, blah blah blah.

And sometimes it works.

Sometimes it works but each and every time a goal is achieved it's usually followed by *'whats next?'*. It hasn't been 5 minutes and already we're moving on to the next goal. Goal setting can be extremely beneficial, but it can suck the joy out of the journey to the thing that's meant to make us happy and fulfilled.

The best example of this for me is my time in comedy. Rather than enjoying the present I was becoming too wrapped up in what's next. Making it. What's bigger? What's better?

Would I rather be on that stage, giving it my all, completely and utterly in the moment, feeling great and possibly *not* get a five-star review . . . or . . . be so laser-focused on getting a five-star review that I lose sight of everything else, stressing myself in the process and not enjoy the performance at all?

Nowadays, when I'm on stage keynoting, my goal is simple; give it my best on that day and come off stage feeling good enough to want to do it all again tomorrow.

Too many of us spend our days feeling discouraged, tired or unmotivated from chasing an endless stream of goals that seem a long way away, so maybe it's time to re-examine the order of things. Or more so, our timescales.

'Beware of Destination Addiction, a preoccupation with the idea that happiness is in the next place, the next job, or with the next partner. Until you give up the idea that happiness is somewhere else, it will never be where you are'.

Robert Holden

So, what is reverse goal setting, why is it great and more importantly, how do we do it?

This is about gaining a different perspective. Flipping the traditional on its head and seeing things through a slightly different lens. Inspired by my Reverse Pumping friend (still funny) we spot different opportunities, find new solutions to problems and along the way all sorts of goals will jump out. Reverse goal setting is less about 'making it' in the old school sense and more about working out a path for yourself that is actually fulfilling, right now.

And best of all, it's really simple.

Ask yourself three questions.

1. What do I want to feel right now?
2. What activity can I do right now to give me that feeling?
3. If I do this activity regularly, what results will it create?

That's it! It's that simple, and once you gain momentum with this, you'll be amazed at just what you achieve.

'What you do frequently becomes your frequency'.

Anon

Let me give you an example. You might say right now, *'I want to feel healthier'*. Ok, what activity allows you to do that? A 30-minute walk outdoors always leaves us feeling better both mentally and physically. So, today you will want to have a 30-minute walk around the block. If you did this every day for six weeks, what sort of result would that create?

It would create a healthier, happier you right from the off! So, if you want to be a healthier, happier you then commit to do something that builds momentum. Before you know it, a 30-minute walk might turn into a 60-minute walk. It might even turn into a run . . . and you might even end up running a marathon two years later but from day one you felt better.

You might say, 'Right now, I would like to feel relaxed'. Magic! Today, what activity makes you relaxed? You might say, '15 minutes of mindfulness makes me feel relaxed, every time I do it, it chills me out a little'. Awesome. So, if you do 15 minutes of mindfulness every day for the rest of your life, what sort of results would that create? There's going to be a far less stressed you walking about and who knows, you might just become a mindfulness master in the process! Imagine how many goals you'll achieve being more relaxed!

Why wait 10, 20, 30 or more years to truly start living? There's no point. You don't have to wait for anything. You can feel the way you want to feel, today. You don't have to postpone you. You don't have to put you off.

No more constant chasing, wishing and hoping for stuff that feels like a lifetime away. Right now, choose the feelings you want to feel, find the activities that give you these feelings and do them.

Every day people wait for 5 p.m. All week they wait for Friday. Don't let the pursuit of tomorrow diminish the joy of today.

That's it. Simple. Get it done.

Putting the Trolley Away

In 2021, as the world remained locked down during the pandemic, a simple idea was posted anonymously online, essentially suggesting a unique way to determine whether you were a good person or not. And like many random things on the internet, it blew up big time and shocked many into reconsidering their behaviours.

Meliorism

(noun) /melya,rizam/-

the belief that we can contribute to positive change and improve the world through acts of love, creativity, compassion and kindness.

Going to the supermarket is not uncommon. At times we might just pop in to grab a couple of items but occasionally life requires a big shop. You may call it the weekly shopping, but in many Scottish people's homes, it's the big shop. And the big shop requires a trolley.

Shopping trolleys (aka 'carts' for my US friends) are the same the world over. We've all seen one, we've all pushed one, we've all filled one, we've all sat in one and we've all lay across the top of one while our friends or siblings push us through supermarket aisles at great speeds.

Haven't we?

You leave with a trolley full of supermarket treasures. You head for the car. You unlock the car, open the boot and hoist all the shopping bags out of the trolley and into the car.

Someone needs to return the trolley. Let's assume this is you.

There's a choice. Either you can return the trolley to the actual supermarket itself, or you can return it to one of the many trolley bays scattered across the car park, designed to make life easier for those of us in a hurry.

It's just that sometimes you find yourself parked a fair distance from said supermarket or said trolley bay.

In this moment, you are faced with dilemma. To return? Or, not to return? That is the question.

And this dear reader, is where it gets interesting . . .

To return the shopping trolley is an easy, convenient task and one which we all recognise as the correct, appropriate thing to do.

To return the shopping trolley is, in its simplest form, the right thing to do. And plus, let's not forget, you'll get your pound coin back!

There are very few reasons to *not* return the trolley. Dire emergencies, young kids in the car or perhaps you are physically unable to, I'll give you all of these but aside from that, returning the trolley is the right thing to do. It doesn't matter that it's someone's actual job to put trollies away. *You* should put the trolley away.

But, it's not illegal to *not* return it. It's not illegal to abandon your trolley in the middle of the car park or on a pavement nearby. No one will punish you. You won't receive a fine, you definitely won't be going to jail and it's no-one is going to kill you.

Therefore, the shopping trolley presents itself as the perfect example of whether a person will do what is right without being forced to do it.

You still with me?

You gain nothing from returning the shopping trolley. In other words, you must return the shopping trolley out of the goodness of your own heart. You must return the shopping trolley because it is the right thing to do. Because it is correct.

The theory claims that the humble shopping trolley is what determines whether a person is a good or bad member of society. Now, some might feel this seems far-fetched or perhaps overly simplistic.

But it stopped me in my tracks.

'There's no guarantee tomorrow will be better. But you can be'.

@ThoughtsFired

The shopping trolley theory for me is representative of so many moments in life where we find ourselves faced with a very simple decision of doing the right thing, or not.

Picking up litter. Tidying your house. Studying for an exam. Waiting in line. Preparing for a job interview. Leaving an unhappy relationship. Getting healthy. Helping your parents. Saying *'thank you'*. I could keep going!

In fact, here's a huge one; picking up dog shit! Not sure if you've noticed? THERE'S DOG SHIT EVERYWHERE! Not quite 'late 1980s everywhere', but still!

Quite often, doing the right thing requires a bit more energy, a bit more effort. But here's the thing, we feel better for doing it. There's always an easier route.

This whole thing is about being in a moment and doing the right thing.

In life we are faced with continuous, daily decision-making dilemmas. If you find yourself presented with one of these moments and you know what the right thing is to do but there is an easier, quicker way, no matter how much more effort is involved, how much more time it will take, just think to yourself *'Put the trolley away'*.

And then I don't get dog shit all over my new retro Pumas!

Not Enough Meat on the Bones

One of the biggest 'Trolley Moments' for me came in my teens; homework and studying for exams.

I reckon I'm the world's best procrastinator. A mighty declaration to make in a world full of procrastinators. I'm not proud of it but I am brilliant at it. Ninja level good. 5th dan procrastinator.

I'm making the assumption here that you know what procrastination means, so apologies if I'm about to patronise you.

Patronise, that's when I tell you something you already know . . . That right there is a very clever joke. Well, in my mind anyway. I'll move on.

Pro-cras-ti-na-tion

noun

the action of delaying or postponing something: your first tip is to avoid procrastination.

So, the question was always 'To study . . . or not to study?' Put the trolley away or just leave it for someone else to worry about? Pick the dog shit up, or leave it for someone to step in? After all, just what could go wrong? Well, I definitely found this out!

Fast forward to today. Mid-40s and still, easily the best procrastinator in Scotland. My ability to put things off is second to none.

In other words, I am a self-confessed world champion puterofferer!

Poo-ter-off-er-er

noun

someone who can't stop looking out the window imagining the seagulls are in fact having a disco, thumbing at Instagram and WhatsApping mates, instead of doing the thing that they're meant to be doing, that they know is proper important.

Sound familiar?

The ability to put things off or certainly leave them to the last minute comes very naturally to me. I have however gotten better with age at combatting this. Big grown-up deadlines with financial implications definitely – at times – provide the boot up the backside often required.

But as a teenager, my ability to leave things such as studying and homework to the last minute was second to none. I didn't enjoy it. I knew it was important and the right thing to do but my head was often up my backside. It was boring.

The result was often a half-assed attempt to produce something passable in record time. Every single parent's night my teachers told my parents the same thing, *'he's capable, there's just not enough meat on the bones'*.

For the record, they also noted I was a 'daydreamer', 'couldn't sit still' and was 'often easily distracted'. I'll come back to this later!

Of course, as the essays got longer and the content more complicated, the greater the level of focus required. It was here my ability to put things off reached new heights. Bear in mind this was pre-social media days.

No SMART phones. No YouTube or TikTok. I reckon throughout my school career I literally spent months pacing my room, creating comedy routines and dreaming up new wallpaper patterns.

Then came four years of university.

I can recall having an assignment due on a Monday morning. I started it on the Sunday evening at 7 p.m. I had been given the work three weeks prior. At 7 p.m., I sat down, picked up a pen and by 10 p.m. I had successfully made an origami swan. I worked entirely from memory after an art lesson nine years previously and genuinely felt a sense of achievement. It was a beautiful swan, but no assignment completed, yet.

The assignment was on Educational Psychology. Not origami. Or swans.

I still got the assignment handed in. And passed. But only just.

I love the way author and speaker Tim Urban writes about the difference between the brain of a procrastinator and that of a non-procrastinator.

He challenges us to imagine both brains having a wee person in them, standing at a ships wheel, steering us through life. Tim calls this wee person our 'Rational Decision Maker'. We all have one.

In both brains, the 'Rational Decision Maker' wants the same thing, and both believe they are able to make good decisions and take appropriate action in life. Again, we all have one.

According to Tim, the main difference between a puterofferer and non-puterofferer is that the brain of a puterofferer is also inhabited by a small primate that he calls the 'Instant Gratification Monkey'.

It was only after reading Tim's work that I was able to finally understand just what was going on in my head. I was 30 years old when I had this breakthrough. 30 . . .

All these years, I've had – in Tim's words – an 'Instant Gratification Monkey' living alongside my 'Rational Decision Maker'.

I have a feeling that right now you're thinking something along the lines of . . . 'What the hell is an Instant Gratification Monkey?'

Let me explain . . .

Basically, the 'Rational Decision Maker' is the sensible voice in your head that says things like 'Now is the perfect time to get some work done. I'm going to sit at my desk and smash that report that needs doing. Put the trolley away!'

'I like work; it fascinates me. I can sit and look at it for hours'.

Jerome K. Jerome

The 'Instant Gratification Monkey' is the other voice in your head that says, *'Ooh look, a squirrel, I'm going to call it Barry, watch him for an hour and wonder what he'd look like in dungarees!'*

Here's the problem, no one's 'Rational Decision Maker' knows the first thing about how to own a monkey. Unfortunately, it wasn't a part of the training, and 'Rational Decision Maker' is left completely helpless as the monkey makes it impossible for anyone to do their job.

Here's the even bigger problem, the 'Rational Decision Maker' doesn't understand the 'Instant Gratification Monkey' and the 'Instant Gratification Monkey' doesn't understand the 'Rational Decision Maker'.

The following is a genuine conversation I had with myself. You can see it clearly demonstrates the work of both my 'Rational Decision Maker' and my 'Instant Gratification Monkey'.

I'm going to join a gym.

But I don't find the gym fun.

It's really good for me, I always feel good after exercise.

It'll hurt and I'll look ridiculous.

I'll do a 5k run instead and then have a big healthy bowl of porridge.

I'll skip my run today, oh look, crisps.

Documentary about Wrestling.

I skipped my run and ate crisps. And I ate them in a sandwich while going down a massive Wrestling wormhole. Don't get me wrong, it was delicious and thoroughly entertaining, but the monkey won. The trolley was well and truly left, abandoned, in the middle of the car park.

The monkey thinks *only* about the present, ignores any lessons learned from previous slip-ups, doesn't even begin to think about the future and what implications this may have. Basically, monkey is all about making sure that right now is lovely and fun and easy.

For monkeys it's easy, eat when you're hungry, sleep when you're tired, don't do anything too difficult and you'll be a pretty successful monkey.

The problem for you and I is that we are human, and we live in the human world. I'm not sure about you but I'm happy to admit that I'm rubbish at fighting monkeys, and the more he's in control, the worse I feel.

It's at this moment we procrastinators spend a lot of time in what Tim Urban calls the 'Dark Playground'. He describes it as *'a place where leisure activities happen at times when leisure activities are not supposed to be happening'.*

In other words, the fun we're having isn't actually fun because deep down you know you've not 'earned' it, and that underlying feeling of guilt, anxiety and dread is slowly but surely building. The thing that you're meant to be doing, that really needs done, will still be there needing done when you've finished pouring through Instagram reels for an hour.

So just how does a procrastinator ever manage to get things done?

For me the answer is pure fear. Tim Urban calls it the 'Panic Monster'. It suddenly wakes up when a deadline is fast approaching or there's any chance whatsoever of being left looking like a fool in public or anything that has any kind of scary consequences.

The Instant Gratification Monkey is terrified of the Panic Monster. Tim nails it when he asks, *'How else could you explain the same person who can't write a paper's introductory sentence over a two-week span suddenly having the ability to stay up all night, fighting exhaustion, and write eight pages?'*

I know from experience this is no way to live. It's awful and you end up selling yourself short, focusing on all things needing done rather than the thing you want to be doing.

So, let's talk about something that plays a huge part in our adult lives, something that can play on our mind and eat away at us. Something that forms the basis of so many (self) conversations and is often the root cause of so much stress and heartache, yet we never seem to prioritise or indeed get round to dealing with them:

Fulfilment and contentment.

Or to be more specific . . . the *lack* of our own fulfilment and contentment.

The Enough Stuff

I used to think fulfilment and contentment were the same thing. They may seem similar, but they're worlds apart in how they shape our lives.

Contentment is that sense of inner calm you get when you're genuinely happy with what you've got, right now, where you feel no need to chase after more. It's all about embracing the moment, finding peace in the present and finding joy in the simple, ordinary experiences.

On the flip side, fulfilment is where the magic happens. It's about achieving a deeper sense of purpose and meaning in life. Fulfilment often comes from pursuing goals, passions, and contributing to something larger than yourself. In essence, contentment is about appreciating the now, while fulfilment is about the satisfaction of living a purposeful life.

'A fulfilled life doesn't point to the number of years, awards, wealth and followers someone amassed for himself, but the number of faces that smiled because of him'.

Michael Bassey Johnson

The secret ingredient here is gratitude. In both cases, gratitude serves as a grounding force, reminding you of the value in your experiences and helping you find peace and purpose in both the present and the journey ahead.

To be truly content and fulfilled in life, not only should we focus on the stuff that makes us happy right now, but the stuff that doesn't, and stop doing them.

Yup, you read that correctly. Take all the things that make you unhappy, and don't do them.

Imagine . . .

The Long Lost Art of 'No'

Saying 'Yes' is easy and your happiness is made up of the choices you make in life. That's quite a bold statement. But saying *'No'* is a bold move. I'll say it again. Your happiness is made up of the choices you make in life.

'If something is not a "hell, YEAH!", then it's a "no!"'

James Altucher

We all know that being on the receiving end of a 'no' can be brutal. But you saying 'yes' to everything won't make up for that.

'No' is a complete sentence. It rarely requires anything after it. It can be used in any situation and it can, at times, feel wonderful.

But so often we feel the need to say 'yes'. Yes to our friends, yes to our parents, yes to our clients, yes to our employer, yes to our teachers, yes to the latest trends, yes to the latest gadgets, yes to someone else's plans at the weekend . . . I could keep going.

And often when we really want to say 'no', we say 'yes' because it's easier than saying 'no' and then trying to justify why. We don't want to hurt anyone's feelings.

This just leads to feelings of regret.

'Learning to step back from urgency culture isn't about ghosting the world and ignoring your responsibilities. It's about learning how to take back part of your life – and part of yourself – so you can prioritise your happiness and stop felling so overwhelmed and undernourished. Let yourself be human instead of forcing yourself to be a machine. Your heart, nervous system and adrenal glands will thank you'.

Cory Allen

I definitely got to a stage in my life where I was finding I had less and less time to focus on the stuff that matters. I'm a people pleaser. Now, there's nothing wrong with wanting to please others and be of help unless it's at the expense of your own happiness. And that's exactly where I had got to.

I look back on my teenage years and I was the same. Sometimes I couldn't think of anything worse than going to a particular person's house or to a particular party, but everyone else was going and I didn't want to be the only one who wasn't. So, often I said yes. I'd go and whilst sometimes I would be glad I went, more often than not I found myself wishing I had had the confidence to say 'no'.

'First rule of might club: never commit to plans'.

Anon

Saying 'no' is great, it's not a crime! Sometimes it's hard but you will have to say 'no' to many things in life in order to say 'yes' to others. Let's call it 'The Joy of No' or JONO for short.

There are so many things in life you can take great pleasure in saying 'no' to. Here's my own #JONO top 10

1. Negative self-talk
2. Perfection
3. Excuses
4. Comparisons
5. Parties
6. Unhealthy food & alcohol
7. Social media
8. Work I don't enjoy
9. Terrible friends
10. My phone

Don't Do It!

Firstly, I love a daily to-do list. I find them useful; they help me keep track of tasks and prioritise things. Crossing things off gives me a sense of accomplishment and motivates me to keep going! And it helps to reduce stress and anxiety as it helps me to feel in control. And yes, I add things I've done throughout the day to just experience the pleasure of scoring it off!

They've been helping people to increase their productivity for centuries and there is more than enough evidence out there to suggest the classic to-do list is *still* effective for getting stuff done.

'The really idle person gets nowhere. The perpetually busy person does not get much further'.

Heneage Ogilvie

According to 'The Busy Person's Guide to the Done List' by Bailey Adams, 50% of to-dos are completed within a day. Not only that, but many are also ticked off within the first hour of being written down.

But, what about the 41% of these to-do list items that are never completed at all? How can we achieve more, by doing less? Simple: focus some of your energy on 'not-to-dos'.

'Not-to-dos?'

Absolutely, let's say 'hello' to your new favourite thing, a *NOT*-to-do list!

This is the opposite of adding more to your plate; rather, it's about identifying those tasks and distractions that drain your time and energy. Picture it as a force field guarding your precious time and wellbeing, keeping out the things that don't serve you.

Examples of things to add to a 'Not-to-do' list might include social media between 6 a.m.–8 a.m. and 6 p.m.–8 p.m. Maybe it's checking emails between 9 a.m. and 11 a.m. Perhaps it's overcommitting to social engagements, allowing yourself to say no to some things! It might be to *not* ignore self-care, if you've got an hour blocked out for a walk, there's zero negotiating!

'Somewhere in the late 20th century we got the idea that busyness is a virtue. We decided that the more activities we can squeeze into our lives, the happier we'll be. What ultimately results, though, is physical and spiritual exhaustion. We jump from one appointment to another, our body and mind racing. We schedule events back to back and overlapping, with no time to rest or reflect. And when we're in one activity, we're either distracted with the thing we've just done or the thing that's coming up. It's not a good way to live'.

Jack Zavada

By jotting down these non-essential activities, you create clarity and focus on what truly matters. It's a simple yet effective strategy for reclaiming control over your schedule and prioritising what aligns with your goals.

As Tim Ferriss writes, not-to-do lists are often more effective than to-do lists for upgrading performance. The reason is simple: what you don't do determines what you can do.

I can't write your list for you, this is personal! But it could be endless so here's some stuff to keep you on track before you create your first-ever not-to-do list!

1. Shit that distracts you and wastes your time.
2. Shit that stresses you out or causes negative emotions.
3. Shit that drains your energy.
4. Shit you feel obliged to do.
5. Shit that doesn't actually need to be done.
6. Shit you can't control or isn't your responsibility.

'It's hip to focus on getting things done, but it's only possible once we remove the constant static and distraction. If you have trouble deciding what to do, just focus on not doing'.

Tim Ferriss

So, it's over to you. Grab a pen, and let's start trimming the fat from our to-do lists. And remember, it might not seem like it at first, but a full life looks very different from a busy life.

Do less, be more.

CHAPTER 7

Head. Clouds. Heart. Sleeve.

I think too many people undervalue their ability to daydream and pass it off as a sort of nothingness that offers them nothing in return.

'I try to maintain a healthy dose of daydreaming to remain sane'.

Florence Welch

My idea of nothing might be different from yours. My nothing is healthy, calm, peaceful, grateful, fulfilled and content, none of which I can claim to be an expert in! Those closest to me would agree that none of these things come naturally to me, some might even say I'm good at exactly none of them. I've always had a difficult relationship with 'nothing' but, for a very particular reason, I am working hard to get better at it.

A lack of patience, focus and my inability to sit still don't help me in my quest but I *want* to get better at it, I want to love it, I certainly want to be able to build more 'nothing' into my day.

My reason for doing so? Daydreaming.

Daydream

Definition: to spend time thinking on pleasant things until you become unaware of your surroundings.

Daydreamer

Definition: someone who spends a great deal of time in their head and getting lost there, for they have a universe inside them.

To be bloody brilliant at daydreaming requires a stillness, the ability to embrace a sense of nothingness and tune out from all and everything around us.

Daydreaming used to come naturally to me. I was *always* good at it, my school reports even said so! But with a busy grown-up life, as for most adults, it doesn't feel as natural as it once did. The sense of calm needed can often feel out of reach.

I recently had to dig out my old school reports from primary school, all part of my own journey of self-discovery and understanding, and for the doctor . . . another story for another day! (IYKYK)

'Gavin is a dreamer'. *'Gavin has a wonderful imagination'*. These phrases feature heavily.

But so do *'He's often in his own little world'*, *'Gavin is easily distracted'* and *'Gavin needs to concentrate more'*.

There are a few *'Gavin always has something to contribute'* and *'Gavin brings lots of energy into the classroom'*.

But there's also a couple of *'Gavin can't sit still'* and *'Gavin talks too much'*.

My school experience was no different from any other child. Some teachers saw me, some didn't.

I wasn't ever into school in a big way. I had good moments, but it was all very distracting to me. I would have a comedy sketch idea in my head, a joke, a script, a character idea, a full-stage production, a song. I paid attention way less than I let on; my daydreaming was next level!

Often derided then, and a staple of many a teacher's report card comments, daydreaming was (and still can be) generally seen as an undesirable activity, especially among school-age children from whom the education system demands unrelenting focus.

But when you're older and a bit more successful, you have 'vision'!

'Keep some room in your heart for the unimaginable'.

Mary Oliver

I don't care who it is, they could be the most dynamic and innovative people in any field, be it business, science, sports, politics or the arts. Obama, Einstein, Curie, Thunberg, Bowie, I don't care how often they are labelled as visionaries. A 'vision', at the end of the day, is just a fancy word for 'daydream' therefore a 'visionary', well, that's just a daydreamer with a posh title!

Let's take all the visionaries, all the successful types who get away with zoning out during meetings because they're 'envisioning the future'. Strip away the fame, the power and the money, and they're doing exactly what you and I did in class (and often still to this day) when we imagined ourselves as a rock star or a superhero instead of listening to yet another lecture on the Battle of Hastings.

Fancy titles don't change the fact that the greatest minds in the world spend a good chunk of their time with their heads in the clouds. What they don't always tell us is that there's a place for you and me.

Nubivagant

[nooby-vah-gant]
Adjective

1. wandering throughout the clouds or amongst the clouds.

Newton was probably chilling under that apple tree, daydreaming about lunch, when gravity hit him (literally). J.K. Rowling was on a train, daydreaming about a young wizard, when Harry Potter popped into her head. Even Einstein was known for his 'thought experiments', which is just science-speak for epic daydreaming sessions.

Like Einstein, Mozart and Da Vinci both scheduled time every day to do nothing. Not brainstorming, not focusing . . . mind wandering.

'*Everything starts as someone's daydream*'.

Larry Niven

We daydream nearly 47% of our waking hours. If our brain spends nearly half of our awake time doing it, there is probably a good reason why.

Visionaries take their daydreams and spin them into something grand. They make the impossible seem possible, turning 'Wouldn't it be cool if . . .' into 'Hey, check this out!'

So, the next time someone catches you staring off into space, just tell them you're honing your visionary skills. After all, behind every great invention, masterpiece or revolutionary idea is a daydream that refused to stay put.

I believe daydreaming is the unsung hero of human creativity. It can be mistaken for laziness, but let's set the record straight: daydreaming is where the magic happens. Imagine a world without daydreamers. We'd still be sitting in caves, staring at rocks, wondering what's for dinner.

I have spent so much of my life in education. I went to wee school as a wee kid, then big school as a big kid, then really big school as a really big kid where I learned to teach the wee kids in the wee school. Then I taught the wee kids in the wee schools and now I run a business that works in all schools with all kids . . . aged 3–103.

If I had a pound for every time I have heard a child being told or have in fact *been* told 'get your head out the clouds', I'd be fucking loaded!

'They said daydreaming was against the law, but some of us escaped, slipping out windows and over cyclone fences, some of us flying away with heads like balloons. We taught our dogs to love the flavour of homework and became expert forgers of our parent's signatures. We knew they were teaching us how to die but some of us said no in our stealthy and stubborn ways'.

Vern Rutsala

We live in a time where we need to get our heads back in the clouds. We need to embrace daydreaming for the superpower it is. When we dare to dream, we forge our future and build a sense of belief, creativity and resilience. It's not luck, it's neuroscience.

See, when your mind wanders, it lights up an area of the brain called the 'default mode network'. This lets you tap into your imagination, emotions and ability to reflect; it's your brain's creative playground.

And let's not forget it's bloody good for us! Good brain health requires regular periods of relaxation. When these periods involve letting our mind wander, it helps reduce stress and anxiety. Mind-wandering is *not* rumination. And daydreaming is not mind-wandering. Daydreaming is 'thinking for pleasure', and as adults it's harder than we think.

When was the last time you had a good, old-fashioned daydream? I mean, the kind you probably mastered as a kid, zoning out and building castles in the sky. Turns out, it's a skill, and many of us are a bit rusty.

Researchers, bless them, tried to coach grownups to think 'meaningful thoughts'. Guess what? We're shit at it; it was a total flop. Not only did the study participants not have the rewarding experience the researchers intended, but they also thought their own unguided thoughts were more pleasant.

Dr Erin Westgate, leading the charge, was baffled at first. Why wasn't meaningful thinking hitting the mark? Turns out, people's 'meaningful' thoughts were heavy, serious stuff. No wonder it wasn't enjoyable! They'd forgotten that daydreaming isn't about solving world hunger or ending wars, it's about letting your mind roam free.

On the other hand, when participants were encouraged to *think for fun*, their minds filled up with visions of 'cake and avocado toast' which, let's be honest, are great but not exactly life changing.

The real magic happened when researchers gave examples of pleasant *and* meaningful things to ponder. Suddenly, people were 50% happier in their daydreaming.

Bottom line, it's not easy and it takes practice. But the payoff? It's like magic. A polished daydreaming habit can boost your mood, soothe stress and maybe even make Mondays less grim. So, go ahead . . . head, clouds, give it a try.

Daydreaming isn't just for kids, it's for all of us. *'This is part of our cognitive toolkit that's underdeveloped, and it's kind of sad'*, says Westgate. But with a bit of effort, you might just rediscover your brain's happiest playground.

Daydreaming fuels confidence. But these are hard times for dreamers, therefore it's not always easy to feel confident.

'You believed in Santa for 10 years, you can believe in yourself for 10 seconds'.

Anon

Helmet Up!

I love my scooter. When I say 'scooter', I mean an actual scooter. Not a moped with an engine. Not an electric scooter, a literal scooter. A kid's one. Except its mine. And I'm in my 40s.

As much as I love scooting, the majority of my scoots are to the wee shop for milk or bread. I've only ever fallen off twice. Once at the skatepark, my son was so mortified, we had to leave and the other was on the way for milk, just me on my own!

Stupidly, I wasn't wearing a helmet. Even on the milk run we need to protect those dreams in that cranium of yours!

I was feeling particularly confident for a non-scooter stunt specialist. I still don't know why but I figured I could do a bit of a jump while going full speed. Not even a spectacular jump, literally a bit of a jump. You may know it as a bunny hop!

I'm not sure if I hit a stone or crack in the pavement but my scooter stopped immediately. I didn't. I went over the top at what felt like 70 miles per hour and hit the ground at what felt like 100 miles per hour. If there was ever a word to describe how I hit the ground, it's 'slam'. The kind of fall that if someone had filmed it, I'd be viral, and the world would laugh together, secretly wondering if I lived.

Imagine a meteor hitting the road, tearing up the tarmac, except I'm the meteor.

'Sucking at something is the first step towards being sorta good at something'.

Jake the Dog, Adventure Time

I'm thinking overconfidence may have had something to do with it. It hurt immensely but not for the first 14 seconds or so. I think I was in shock, and I was fully winded, you know the kind of winded that prevents you from breathing, but you make a horrendously loud 'UUUUUUUUUUUUUUH' noise? That.

But it didn't matter, I had 14 seconds until the agony set in, I was up like a shot, blood pouring from my arms, dreams intact (luckily no head knocks) and fled the scene hoping exactly none of the neighbours had witnessed my catastrophic (pathetic) attempt at what can only be described as one of the lesser, perhaps more amateur stunts.

I had milk to get.

The thing is, sometimes our confidence can get us in trouble.

Did you know that 8% of males and 7% of females think they could beat a lion in a fistfight? Actually true! This is definitely the kind of confidence that's going to get people in trouble.

We're told all through life from a very young age that confidence is key. The way one carries themselves, acts, stands, walks, talks and interacts with others. How you walk into the exam hall, that job interview or the first time you ask someone out, confidence matters. There even comes a day they tell us that confidence is an attractive trait for humans to have.

That explains why I was rubbish at school with exams *and* girls!

The thing is, there's believing in yourself and then there's downright delusion. Believing you can make a brilliant cheese toastie is confident, believing you can beat a lion in a fight is hilarious.

We all know someone who could be described as *over*confident. But is overconfidence really a thing, can we actually be *too* confident? Can confidence actually become a hindrance?

And, perhaps more importantly, what about those of us who lack confidence? Does it mean that unless we are bursting with confidence, we don't stand as good a chance as our peers at achieving our dreams?

Are those of us who perhaps struggle with confidence also allowed to aim for the clouds or does this now make us overly confident too?

I'm confused.

Just as well the experts at the Institute for the Psychology of Elite Performance at Bangor University have extensively examined this very thing.

The reason I'm into this is I struggle with confidence. You've probably realised by now that my heart is firmly on my sleeve, so I'm very comfortable sharing this with you. It's a bit like when people hear about my struggles with anxiety, they don't always believe it because of my job. They see me on stage, remember my stand-up days, or read my books, and naturally think I've got it all together. But the truth is, I doubt myself constantly. I'm always questioning and second-guessing myself, and it drives me nuts. So yeah, I'm really interested to hear what the experts have to say.

Firstly, what exactly is low confidence?

'I'm the best there is! Except maybe for that guy . . . and that guy . . . and that guy . . .'

SpongeBob SquarePants

Low confidence is that nagging feeling that we're not ready to tackle what's ahead. Sound familiar? That's me, constantly. It was me throughout school, and it's me now, pacing backstage, questioning why I'm here and why anyone would care to listen.

So, what happens when we lack confidence?

Well, we either bail on the task – clearly not ideal – or we double down and put in extra effort.

Not all bad, right?

In one study, participants were asked to skip with a rope for a minute. Then, they were told to do it again with a supposedly more difficult rope (spoiler: it was the same rope). The results? Confidence dropped, but performance actually improved.

So, self-doubt can be beneficial?

Exactly. It can push us to be better, to try harder and to put in more effort. We try harder.

Now let's consider the role of overconfidence. A high level of confidence is usually helpful for performing tasks because it can lead you to strive for difficult goals. But high confidence can also be detrimental when it causes you to lower the amount of effort you give towards these goals.

Overconfidence often makes people no longer feel the need to invest all their effort, think of that person you knew who studied less for upcoming exams at school.

Interestingly, research shows that when you believe you are better than you really are, it will have a negative effect on whatever the task is at hand and your performance essentially dips.

Unfortunately, there is another common side effect to overconfidence, referred to in the science community as *Dicketh-headethness*. Again, we all know one.

So, this is good news for those of us who lack confidence but still care enough to want to do well and give our all in life . . . and maybe even dare to be successful at something.

Get your head back in the clouds, it's good for you, that you can be confident of, don't give up the daydream, lean in and never ever cover that heart on your sleeve . . .

Jackets Off

Throughout my life and career, I've often been labelled an 'over-sharer'. Personally, I find this term somewhat derogatory. Interestingly, back in my school days, some teachers described me differently on my report cards: 'Gavin wears his heart on his sleeve'. I think this feels kinder but this contrast between negative and positive perceptions has been a recurring theme in my journey.

From childhood to my professional life, the perception of being transparent with my emotions has followed me. It's a trait I hear about frequently, viewed both positively and negatively. While some see it as a sign of openness and authenticity, others may perceive it as a vulnerability or oversharing. This contrast in perspectives continues to intrigue me. It's as if my openness and transparency are perceived differently depending on the context and the observer's mindset.

'Having a soft heart in a cruel world takes courage not weakness'.

Katherine Henson

I don't choose to wear my heart on my sleeve, it's not been a conscious decision. It's not something I have worked hard at, I simply don't know how to be any other way, I don't know how to do things differently.

Why would I not talk about my mental health? Why would I not talk about my family? Why would I not talk about my failures? Why would I not talk about the awful way in which my dad died? All these things make me, me.

What I have had to do is get comfortable with me. I *was* comfortable with me, until society taught me differently! I have had to not only accept but embrace this is who I am. Some call it vulnerability. Cool, I'm down with that.

Every time I feel anxious about being 'too much', I think about when the Mad Hatter tells Alice, *'You've lost your muchness. You used to be much muchier'*.

What I've also had to do is get comfortable with other people *not* being comfortable with people like me. Society appears to still have an issue with humans displaying their vulnerability. It can at times still be perceived as weakness.

But in a world often fixated on strength and success, I've recently become aware of a quiet revolution happening, one that celebrates vulnerability as a strength. Far from weakness, I'd go as far to say vulnerability may now be the hallmark of authenticity and courage. Someone even told me it's cool. It's not just cool; it's transformative.

People are hungry for something real. In a world overflowing with fake food, fake news, fake followers and artificial everything, the most powerful thing you can be is unapologetically, wholeheartedly, *you.*

Perhaps most importantly, the magic of vulnerability is that it's utterly liberating. It frees us from the pressure to appear flawless, allowing us to celebrate our journey, scars and all. It encourages growth, as we confront our fears and embrace new possibilities. I spent years of my life trying to fit in, wondering why I don't feel comfortable. I realise now some of us are designed to fit out.

'There's magic in people who aren't afraid to be a little weird, sometimes messy, but always real. They choose to shine their light instead of dimming it to fit in.

These are rare souls who bring sunshine with them wherever they go, and who can trip over their own feet and call it a dance. They've realised that a secret to living a life of joy is to embrace being a hot mess of happiness instead of trying to be perfect'.

Anon

I find something admirable about the ones who wear their hearts on their sleeve. As Danielle Lesik beautifully expresses, it is us who take in the world at its lowest, see it for what it is and dare to love it anyway.

As I have learned to balance my emotions and rationale, I now find pleasure in wearing my heart, my story and my hopes on my sleeve.

'Work of sight is done. Now do heart work on the pictures within you'.

Rainer Maria Rilke

Would I go as far to say it's a gift? That's a tough one to answer.

If a gift can leave you feeling drained and incredibly sad, then yes. If a gift can cloud good days and fill us with false hope, then yes. If a gift can make others uncomfortable, then yes. If a gift can leave you feeling utterly alone and misunderstood, then definitely 100% it's a gift.

We might be seen as childish, or dramatic, but we are the feelers in a world of thinkers. We pour our souls into others to find joy. We are the caregivers who give all that we have in order to feel good.

Our vulnerability is our strength, and our capacity to love deeply is what makes us extraordinary. In our authenticity we bring light. We are beacons. Glimmers.

We're bold, we venture into the unknown, fuelled by hope, passion and the belief that the treasures worth finding aren't always hidden beneath the surface.

The Detectorists

Sometimes we find all of the above in the unexpected, like a TV show. But, sometimes, a TV show isn't just a TV show; it's a gentle tap on the shoulder reminding you what truly matters. The *Detectorists* is exactly that, a beautiful, heartwarming meditation on the ordinary moments we so often overlook. It's not about shiny treasures but the rusty, weathered joys of friendship, hope and purpose.

Have you seen it?

If you are overwhelmed with the current state of the world or struggling to switch off your thoughts, allow yourself time to absorb this wee beauty.

I stumbled across *The Detectorists* when I was at my lowest, when my mind was a whirlwind of anxiety, and everything felt out of control. It's not a big-budget blockbuster or the kind of series that shouts for attention, but that's exactly why it worked its magic on me. Each night, with my wife and son, I'd watch an episode. It became part of my package, and bit by bit, I started to breathe again.

Set against the idyllic English countryside, the series follows Lance and Andy, two metal detectorists searching for lost artifacts but finding much more along the way. The beauty lies in its simplicity, it's a masterclass in mindfulness, where every shot of swaying grass, the music, and every understated joke whispers, *slow down, notice this, this is life.*

I can honestly say that this show has been a fundamental part of my journey.

There's something profoundly calming about it, the gently rolling fields, the hum of metal detectors, the unspoken bond of two friends sharing a flask of tea under a wide, open sky. This show simply invites you to just *be.* It's about searching, yes, but it's not the gold or the ancient coins that matter. It's the connection, the patience, the joy of small discoveries. Glimmers.

The *Detectorists* doesn't hit you over the head with its wisdom. It just gently reminds you there's treasure all around if you know how to look for it.

A show that makes you feel this good really is a precious thing. It's a sunkick, and it's worth leaning into!

Plight of the Humble *Be*

Maybe we need to get back to basics. The simple things. The stuff we don't consider so much anymore because our minds are so full up with modern day, grown-up shite.

As a professional speaker, aside from 'Do you still get nervous?', there's one question I get asked more than any other: 'What are your top tips?'. It's the holy grail, isn't it? Everyone wants that elusive secret. Confidence in a bottle. A magic spell to smash it on stage, to not be nervous, to actually enjoy the moment, to just . . . *be.*

'Wherever you are, be there totally'.

I rarely use any slides at all during my talks. No one has ever complained. In fact, quite the opposite. It's easy to fall into the trap of believing that slides are a necessary component of public speaking.

But they're not.

Too often, we spend hours perfecting our slides instead of honing our speaking skills. But the true power of a presentation lies in the speaker, not the visuals.

Same in actual real life with actual real humans. As I mentioned in Chapter 5, people are looking for the secret to life. A silver bullet to success. True power lies in the actual person, not a job title, not an image, not a fancy car or any other superficial nonsense. Remember, the secret is that there is no secret!

Contrary to popular belief, confidence isn't some mythical power and there's no 'one size fits all'. Confidence is personal and it's beautifully unique. And let's be honest, no one has it all figured out. Not me, not you, not Taylor Swift. (Okay, maybe Taylor.)

I've lost count of how many times I've banged on about the ability to 'just be' in this book. Seriously, *how many times?* And while we're counting, I hope you've realised it's not just a throwaway phrase. This isn't fluff, its life changing.

'Unease, anxiety, tension, stress, worry – all forms of fear – are caused by too much future, and not enough presence. Guilt, regret, resentment, grievances, sadness, bitterness, and all forms of non-forgiveness ate caused by too much past, and not enough presence'.

Eckhart Tolle

This book of course isn't about public speaking. It was going to be, but hey, shit happens. And my goodness did shit happen! Life isn't about smashing it in front of an audience or wooing the room with dazzling charisma (Lol). Nope, it's so much more.

This book has become something else, and it will mean something different to everyone. Perhaps for some it's an exploration of what it means to live authentically in a world that constantly demands more, bigger, better, louder? Maybe for others it's about the delicate balance between striving and being, between ambition and self-acceptance?

Or about how to embrace your quirks, own your imperfections and show up in the world without shouting about it? Or even a rallying cry for the quiet achievers, the thoughtful doers, and the people who don't need to be the loudest in the room to make an impact?

Maybe for some it's a not-so-deep dive into the pressure of being everything to everyone, tackling burnout, people-pleasing and the constant comparison trap. And maybe – just maybe – it encourages readers to carve their own path while staying true to themselves.

Part memoir, part self-help and part self-hell, Confidently Lost might be a gentle challenge to rethink how we show up in the world when we feel out of sorts.

Someone described it as a manifesto for embracing gallusness with humility. I like that. Daring to be bold without hurting others, balancing self-assurance with kindness, and finding joy in simply *being*.

For some, it's the first time they'll realise it's going to be ok.

Learning to 'just be' isn't about stepping onto a stage. It's about stepping into *yourself*. Into *life*. It's about being present, being human and being unapologetically, brilliantly *you*.

Gav, do you have top tips or not?

Ok ok, but let me start with a reminder/disclaimer: there are no rules to life, or public speaking for that matter. None. Zero.

Well, maybe one . . . 'Don't be a Dick'.

Life doesn't come with a manual, and anyone who tells you otherwise is probably trying to sell you something. Public speaking *does* tend to come with one, but it's mostly nonsense and again, it's usually from someone trying to sell you something.

But if there *were* rules – just for argument's sake – here's my list. Take it, leave it, scribble it on a napkin. These aren't commandments, but they're a damn good place to start.

To Be or Not to Be Rules (for Life, and public speaking . . .)

1. **Be nervous** – Embrace the nerves. Enjoy them. Accept them. Own them. Love them. This is who you are. Fidget. Pace, sweat if you must. And as you walk out your front door (or on stage), big deep breath and remember who the fuck you are!

2. **Be real** – Heart on the sleeve, always. Honest. Kind. Genuine. Authentic. Truthful. It's your skin you're in, own it, all of it, even the looser bits, get comfortable with it. Humans relate, connect and respond to truth and passion. They feel it. You feel it. Love.

3. **Be weird** – Embrace it. Authentic. Creative. Innovative. Stand out. The world needs new perspective. Stand/sit/move how you want. Wear what you want. Conventional is easy. Normal is boring. Weird gets remembered.

4. **Be flawed** – Perfect doesn't exist, it's a lie. A chance to learn. Opportunity to grow. Authentic (again). Vulnerability is cool. Creates connection. Gains wisdom. Garners support. Seeks guidance. Human.

5. **Be different** – In with the in-crowd? No thanks! Fit out. Blend out. Your uniqueness is who you are. It's in your thoughts, your words, your actions. People will notice. Being different helps you make a difference. Purpose.

6. **Be gallus** – Brings clarity. Motivation. Self-worth. True to self. Pure. Pure bold. Pure daring. Pure awesome. Pure brave. Pure rad. Pure adventurous. Pure fun. Pure funny. Pure dead gallus by the way.

7. **Be magical** – Different qualities are welcomed. Lifts any day (or event). A sense of wonder. Mystery. Enchanting. Make life an experience for all. Interact. Perform if you wish. Delight your people. Move others. Imagination is your superpower, use it for good. Connect with the inner child. Shazam.

8. **Be silly** – Playfulness. Good for the soul. Bonding. Positivity. Fun. Removes barriers, creates connection. Reduces pressure on everyone, especially you. Creates smiles. Silliness equals creativity. Happiness. Humour. Joy. Spontaneity. Clever is good but silly is wonderful. Laughter is the best medicine. Mental health.

9. **Be brave** – Embrace the fear. Fuck up. Make mistakes, own them. Shit yourself with pride (context is key). Inspiring. Contagious. Builds confidence and courage. Empowers others. Masters emotions, feels great! Alive.

10. **Be you** – Authentic (Again, again). Genuine. Values driven. Purpose led. Focus. Direction. Say yes. Say no. Boundaries. Your face won't always fit. You're not everyone's cup of tea, accept and enjoy. Avoid cliques. It's your story, tell it. Lean in. Don't be a dick.

The Bottom Line

Remember when you were five and your teacher announced to the class that she/he needed a volunteer to take a note to another class down the corridor?

OMFG!!! To be chosen was just an absolute honour.

Such a simple, everyday ask! And yet, the passion with which it was undertaken, the sheer joy that accompanied this honour, the smile that adorned our faces as we walked along the corridor . . . absolute magic.

I can even remember having a sneaky peek at the note one day and it read 'Gavin, we know you read these'. Absolutely shat myself!

Kids have the most natural ability to lean into life. I can recall a discussion from my student-teacher days with a colleague in the staffroom. I was young and inexperienced but that didn't stop me being utterly inspired by the sheer energy and playfulness the kids gave off at the simplest of tasks.

My colleague told me she referred to them as 'One Buttock Learners'. I had no idea what she was on about.

'Describe their excitement', she said.

'They can't sit still, they're so excited they practically hang off their seats!' I replied.

'Correct. And have you ever seen one fall?'

'Nope'.

'Exactly, they may wobble, but they're always holding on with one buttock!'

I learned years later from my friend, Dr Andy Cope that the phrase 'One Buttock Learner' was coined by composer, Ben Zander.

Zander highlights a fascinating phenomenon in young musicians: the initial grind, the struggle through endless scales and off-key notes, where I and many others choose to quit. But then there are those who persevere, who dig in and connect with their music in a profound way. These are the ones who experience the magic, suddenly, they're not just playing on two buttocks; they're 'one-buttock players', lifted by sheer passion and engagement, and they lean in!

It's as if young kids apply it to their lives almost daily. And then we get older, we struggle to embrace the grind, stay committed, and leaning in seems a touch more uncomfortable. Painful in some cases, literally.

As hard as it is, and with all the energy it requires, what if we chose to lean into those dark difficult moments too? When we skip the hard stuff, it's like sticking to easy levels in a game, its safe, but boring. Those are the moments where we learn what we're made of. When life gets hard, it's very difficult to coast. When we lean into the mess, we discover resilience we didn't know we had, strengths we've barely scratched, and even humour in the madness.

Every struggle you face is a chance to level up, to get sharper and to own your story. Life's not meant to be lived on two buttocks, that would be way too comfortable. Lean forward, take the hit, feel the burn and watch how your toughest moments can flip into your biggest strengths.

Life *should* lift you, right off your seat. Leaning in is for *life* not just for kids. And, as a new call to action, whatever your journey currently looks like, no matter how tough or dark things feel right now, add it to your to-do list today, I challenge you to live a one-buttock life.

Hi, Mum!

waves

CHAPTER 8

Who the Fuck Are the Joneses?

To some, there is something worse than physical death, and that is *social* death.

Welcome to the world of the Joneses, a metaphorical clan that seems to set the standard for success, happiness and achievement. You know who they are, right? The ones we *must* keep up with. The ones with the perfect jobs, the immaculate homes, the holidays, the cars, the social media following and the flawless families.

Guess what?

They're not even fucking real! They don't exist.

'Wanting to be someone else is a waste of who you are'.

Kurt Cobain

The Joneses are a construct, a benchmark against which we measure our own lives, often to our detriment. Complete dicks, they rob us of joy, contentment and fulfilment. They turn our lives into a race where we're constantly chasing an elusive ideal, forgetting to appreciate our own unique journey.

To make it worse, there are loads of them, they're everywhere; your street, your work, your school, your Instagram, your TikTok, your Facebook, your TV.

Except, they're not, are they? I'll tell you where they exist ... IN YOUR HEAD.

Don't take it personally, there are plenty of Joneses living in my head too! I'm slowly evicting them one by one. It's taking a little longer than I'd hoped but I'm getting there.

'You wouldn't let an asshole live in your house, so why let them live in your head?'

Anon

'Keeping Up With The Joneses' was a popular comic strip created in 1913. This comic ran for over 20 years and depicted the day-to-day lives of the McGinis family. The McGinis's strived to always be in competition with their neighbours, the Joneses. When the Joneses brought home a new car, the McGinis family were in the showroom next day.

Our social-climbing obsession through material goods is what has kept this phrase alive for decades since the comic ended. Some people prefer to call it 'spending money you don't have to buy things you don't need to impress people you don't like'.

The root of unhappiness is comparing yourself to others. If you're unhappy now and think more money or success will change that, realise it won't. You will just find a new group of people to compare yourself.

Keeping up with the Joneses simply means you're constantly preoccupied with your standard of living and how it appears to the outside world. This is done through comparison, envy, jealousy and often spending beyond your means.

Next time you find yourself trying to keep up with the Joneses, remember, they're nobody. Unlike them, your journey is real, this is about discovering who *you* are, writing *your* narrative and blowing your own goddamn mind for a change!

Fuck the Joneses!

Care Thinkfully

There's a big difference between caring about *people* and caring about people's *opinions*. There's also a big difference between caring about the *right* people's opinions and caring about *all* the people's opinions! Over the years I have invested a lot of time in *all* the people's opinions. Way too much time. I think as humans we do this naturally, but it doesn't serve us well.

Seriously though, no one is thinking about you nearly as much as you think they are. Take social media as an example. Almost no one gives a fuck about your posts, just as you don't give a fuck about theirs. For sure you get the 'likes' or 'views' occasionally and perhaps your friends leave a lovely little comment, but honestly no one really cares about your day, your dog, your holiday or your exhausting job. And don't get me started on why we even feel the need to post anything in the first place?!

Are we rooting for a job with the Joneses?

It's absolutely crazy how social media has convinced us that 15 likes isn't enough. Imagine 15 people in real life telling you that you looked good or that you'd done a good job, made a good joke or made a good point. This shouldn't seem weird; it should be the norm!

'We're all going to die, all of us, what a circus! That alone should make us want to love each other but it doesn't. We are terrorised and flattened by trivialities, we are eaten up by nothing'.

Charles Bukowski

For real, I might even say you don't matter. I mean, you *do* matter in real life, but not as much as you think. That doesn't sound right, I'm not being nasty, I'm being good, with a twist. Think about it, what I'm saying is people are far too worried about themselves to pay attention to what you're doing! Therefore, often we get caught in a trap with our thinking.

Actually, there are two traps we need to avoid:

1. Caring what they think.
2. Thinking that they care.

And when we let go of that shit, good things happen. But the modern world doesn't make it easy . . .

Fucktose Intolerant

/ˈfʌk.təʊs ɪnˈtɒl.ər.ənt/

noun

A chronic and incurable condition marked by an absolute inability to digest or endure other people's bullshit.

Common side effects may include eye rolling, boundary setting and sudden urges to delete WhatsApp groups.

(Not recognised by the NHS. Yet.)

Finding NEMO

So, you might be curious about how a Disney movie is relevant here. Well, as you'll soon discover, this NEMO is quite different from that Nemo, and even though I had no intentions to talk about the movie, the more I've thought about it, the more I realise that *Finding Nemo* is definitely worth a visit first.

In fact, I love a good Disney and Pixar movie. They rarely fail, from the extraordinary animation and wonderful characters to the heart-warming stories and life-enhancing messages, they've got it all, and they're damn good at it.

Every single Disney/Pixar movie has the same award-winning ingredients . . .

Hero
Sidekick
Villain
Magic
Transformation
Music
Love
Risk
Sacrifice
Setbacks
Happy endings.

Look at the list again, it's basically the recipe for life!

Let's explore *Finding Nemo* before we turn our attention to finding NEMO . . . trust me, it will make sense shortly!

You don't need to be a fan of this movie to not only see but *feel* it's profound takeaways.

Whilst Nemo is very young in this film, it's not a million miles away from a life we've all experienced. For example, Dad's a bit embarrassing and we know Nemo should be listening to him more but at the exact same time we know that Marlin (Nemo's Dad) needs to just learn to trust his child more and discover life for himself.

Weirdly familiar!

And whilst the 'parents just want what's best for you' messages are strong, the biggest takeaways of all are around trust and letting go of the things that hold us back. There's a great moment in the film where Dory and Marlin are inside the whale and Dory is translating what the whale is saying.

'He says it's time to let go. Everything's gonna be alright'.

'How do you know something bad isn't gonna happen?' replies Marlin.

'I don't!'

The whole film is essentially based on the idea of trusting that if we let go, all will be ok.

In the film, Nemo disappears. In real life, one of the most horrendous, panic-inducing moments in life is when you are five years old, you're at the supermarket with your parents and you turn away for all but 10 seconds, only to turn back and realise your parents are no longer there. They're only in the next aisle but until you discover this, it's horror movie time!

As a parent, I can tell you there is only one thing worse than this and it's when you're in the supermarket – or any other busy place for that matter – with your child, you turn away for all but 10 seconds, only to discover . . . your phone is no longer in your pocket! Horror movie time.

I'm joking, of course.

But let's be honest, the moment you think you've lost your phone is quite something, right? The tremor of terror that runs through your entire being, ripping across your chest, around your heart, through the stomach, and down into your legs. The blood instantly drains from your face, and you need to sit down and learn to breathe again.

Other than the supermarket moment above, and anxiety of course, there's not much to rival that feeling when you think you've lost your phone.

Okay, let's talk about the other NEMO . . .

A few years ago, I wrote about JOMO (the Joy of Missing Out) being touted as the next big trend. Many of you may have experienced it, but for so many, it's becoming increasingly difficult to let go of the things that consume us. It's hard to put our phones down, stop comparing our lives to others and simply be present and content.

We only experience what we pay attention to; we only remember what we pay attention to. OUR LIVES ARE WHAT WE PAY ATTENTION TO.

Allow me to introduce a new concept: NEMO. And finding NEMO could be the ultimate solution.

NEMO stands for 'Not Entirely Missing Out' and represents a balanced approach between FOMO (Fear of Missing Out) and JOMO. While FOMO can be unhealthy and JOMO might be unrealistic, NEMO offers a middle path.

Looking again at social media, for example. NEMO allows you to reduce frustrations, negativity and the need for validation while still staying somewhat connected. This way, you can use social platforms positively without feeling overwhelmed. And you'll sleep better!

'Let your phone die once in a while. Let your soul charge instead'.

Anon

Embracing NEMO is about finding a healthier, happier balance and it's entirely achievable.

How?

By taking a whale's advice, of course: letting go and trusting that everything will be okay.

'So you're telling us to take life advice from a whale, in a Disney movie, about a fish?'

Yes. Yes, I am.

'So what exactly should we be letting go of, Gav?'

Well, it's funny you should ask . . .

The Art of Letting Go

Letting go? This is not about giving up or waving the white flag. Quite the opposite, this is about reclaiming your energy and focus. It's an exhilarating leap into a life filled with authenticity, peace of mind and endless potential.

'If the only reason you're not doing something is because of how it might make other people feel, you're going to people-please yourself to death'.

Lauren Mayberry (Chvrches)

But letting go of things that hold us back is a real skill, and it takes practice. Social media has taken a whole bunch of things that have always plagued humans and successfully managed to elevate them to a whole new level of 'Holding us back'.

These include my lifelong friend, self-doubt. Not sure if you've ever met them? Along with self-doubt you may also have met a few other pals of mine; judgement, perfectionism, non-friends, jealousy, bitterness, procrastination, fear, regret, worry, people pleasing and entitlement. Each one stands strong on its own but together they form one almighty gang. And this gang causes nothing but trouble.

Let's start with where much of this stems from, and I warn you now dear reader, it's a biggie; Comparisonitis.

'Sometimes you're ahead, sometimes you're behind. The race is long, and in the end, it's only with yourself'.

Baz Luhrmann, Everybody's Free (To Wear Sunscreen)

Let's just all agree right from the off that it's hard *not* to compare yourself to others. It didn't start with the invention of social media. From a young age we look at others and we notice what they have, what they look like, who they hang out with, where they go on holiday and so on.

We're social creatures, we're primed to fit in, it's almost impossible at times to *not* compare our own lives to that of others.

'This is the great irony of social media: the more you immerse yourself in it, the more lonely and depressed you become'.

Jonathan Haidt

While comparisonitis may go back to the beginning of time, with dinosaurs walking the earth getting upset because Gareth the Triceratops had nicer shoes than everyone else, for me it was in high school that I really began to feel it.

Back then, there was no social media, just teenagers and the school yearbook. I eagerly anticipated its arrival each year, flipping through every page; sports teams, best-dressed teacher, class photos, and those individual headshots with their quirky captions. I couldn't help but compare myself to everyone. It was all about who looked handsome, pretty or just plain weird. Every hairstyle, smile, outfit and posture became a point of comparison.

Our yearbook was like an old-school pre-Facebook Facebook, an annual showcase of social comparisons. It was our very own Comparefest, laid out on paper for all to scrutinise. At least no one could click 'like' or leave a shitty comment below the photos.

'Your grave won't list your follower count'.

Anon

I don't mind telling you that I would sit there thinking 'Look at that weirdo'. 'I wish I looked like him'. 'Who's that?' 'He's a bully, why do all the girls like him?' 'I wish she knew who I was'. 'His gran clearly cut his hair'. 'She's a dick'. 'Who wears that?!' 'I hate them!'

And on it went. But of course, it was all done with innocence, I had no idea what social comparison was. And perhaps more importantly, I kept it to myself . . . I'll come back to this particular point shortly.

Social comparisons are 'me-versus-you' interactions, not 'me-with-you' or 'me-and-you' interactions. And so, I was projecting my fears, shortcomings and inadequacies.

But of course, you get to know people much better as your high school years roll on. It wasn't really until I left school that I realised how wrong I was about some people at my school. Some that I considered mates were in fact just narcissistic arseholes and some that I considered 'uncool' or 'not my kind of person', well, it turns out they were the coolest of all.

As for me, well, I've no idea what people thought of me, but I can tell you they were probably wrong. Very few knew the real me at school. No one knew or understood the depths of my anxiety, almost no one knew I spent hours writing scripts and sketches, dreaming of the stage. I tried my best to fit in with the 'in crowd' and if that meant pretending to be someone I wasn't, then guilty as charged. Fuck it was tough.

Like most, I eventually learned that there's no such thing as an 'in-crowd' and if anyone out there believes they are part of a social group that are better than any other group of humans simply because of the way you look or where you're from then you can fuck right off.

And then Mark whatshisname from Facebook came along and changed the social comparison goalposts. He gave the world a gift. The gift of a never-ending, modern-day, high school reunion from hell.

'Simply muting and blocking common sources of "this makes me feel bad" and asking yourself "is this helping me or anyone", can help you streamline your experience in a positive manner'.

Dr Ben Janaway

No longer was this an annual thing that appears in a book, but a daily one that appears in the palm of our hand. No longer just one picture to look at but EVERYTHING. Hours spent scrolling, clicking, looking and of course, comparing.

And then the floodgates opened with Twitter, Instagram, Snapchat, TikTok, etc. etc. . . .

I've said it in previous books, and I'll say it again, social media can make me feel unwell. It makes being peers difficult. Not just for teenagers but all of society. It can be a horrible place to be. I would ban it if I could.

It's safe to say we now well and truly live in the age of envy and thanks to the invention of social media there's now an envy for everything. But there are levels!

'It's better to be real than perfect'.

Anon

Magazines (remember them?) are definitely responsible for introducing the world to the basics of envy on a mass scale – Level 1: face, body, clothes and hair.

Enter body dysmorphia.

'Winnie the Pooh didn't rock a crop top our whole childhood just to watch us become unconfident in our bodies'.

Anon

Facebook brought us Level 2: houses, holidays, dinners.

Enter a new level of envy.

Instagram moved us to defcon Level 3: everything at once. All of it.

Enter the selfie.

Selfies, eh? They're daft, aren't they? It's a modern paradox, seeking validation through our phones while losing touch with the raw, imperfect beauty of spontaneity.

It's like a cosmic mirror reflecting our desire to be seen and accepted. For sure snap away but remember to laugh at the absurdity of posing for yourself and others. Just never forget to embrace your weirdness, for it's in our quirks that true authenticity often shines brightest.

Oh, and the pouting . . .

Everyone's at it these days, mimicking trends to feel attractive. But the pout has endured. Sultry you say? Nope! It's really weird when you think about it, people are masking insecurity with their lips. Their actual lips!

Deep down, we all know it's ridiculous, most will never say it out loud but it's a desperate attempt to fit in, again sacrificing authenticity for fleeting approval.

It's a *manufactured* moment, within a *real* moment, that you're *not* in! Read that again.

Basically, as you retake your photo, of yourself (still daft) over and over again, you're missing everything around you in that moment.

Embracing and accepting our natural expressions would actually be more empowering, but fear of judgement keeps the pout epidemic alive and reduces genuine smiles to rare gems.

I vote for real smiles; pure magic and utterly infectious!

Imagine if social media closed at the end of a day, like a shop. God it would be great. People would have to talk, go outside, connect, listen to music, read, make art, relax! I can't help but feel the world would be a better place. 6 p.m. . . . the craziness stops.

Unpopular opinion: I would ban it outright. Yup, get rid of it. Shut it down, all of it.

'Deleting all my mental health to focus more on my social media'.

Boinki82

Let's return to envy for a moment, I once overheard someone saying that 'envy rots the bones of contentment'. It's a perfect summation, instead of fueling inspiration, envy brings a bitterness and a resentment with it.

Even though we know it's not real, even though at a *logical* level we all know that images are filtered, and that people are presenting the very best take on their lives, on an *emotional* level, it's still pushing our buttons.

'Some poor, phoneless fool is probably sitting next to a waterfall somewhere totally unaware of how angry and scared he's supposed to be'.

Duncan Trussell

Authenticity is scarce in the social sphere, where millions strive to prove their worth and before we know it, our own lives become a dazzling, flawless charade.

Psychologists highlight the plight of teenagers, but the allure of comparison affects us all. So why do we perpetuate this cycle of posting, sharing and comparing?

William Deresiewicz aptly labels us as sheep, echoing behaviours that may not serve our true selves. Social media's allure lies in its power to influence, but its pitfalls lie in mimicking superficial ideals.

That awkward moment when the internet goes down and you don't know what to do with your life.

Finding DORY

You guessed it, this DORY is different from *that* Dory! And just in case you've been living under a rock these last few years, *Finding Dory* is the superb sequel to *Finding Nemo*. It's not often sequels get it right, but this one is superb. Dory is a very optimistic and kind, but ditzy and forgetful fish. This is because she suffers from short-term memory loss. However, she has a heart of gold and is willing to go to great lengths to help those she loves.

It's a lovely film and like its predecessor has so much to offer when it comes to life and how we see the world. Or perhaps more importantly, how the world sees us. It's rammed full of life lessons that apply to us all, lessons that truly make a difference. All of which we already know but perhaps in this modern social media-led era, like Dory, we've forgotten. Maybe we spend so much time now wrapped up in the 'Unreal' world that we've forgotten just what's important.

For me, there are five big takeaways in this movie that we all need to be reminded of sometimes.

Nobody is perfect and that's ok – Literally nobody, it's time to believe it.

Never lose hope – People are great. Life is great. Things work out.

There's always another way – You might not be used to it. You might not like it, but it doesn't make it wrong.

Don't forget to enjoy the view – Life zips by. Be sure to take it all in. Don't wish your time away.

Just keep swimming – This is an important one. Life throws a lot of shit at us. It's important to keep going.

So many of us have forgotten these five things. So many, like Dory have lost their way. I introduced you earlier to NEMO (Not Entirely Missing Out) and while I believe it's a good way to go, may I now introduce DORY; Discovery of the Real You.

Finding NEMO *and* finding DORY. Just like the movies, together they are a formidable partnership, and with it comes adventure, excitement, trust, love, new friends and a huge amount of fun . . . it just works!

It's not always an easy journey to go on, but given the right amount of time and energy, it is entirely worth the effort.

'Offline is the new luxury'.

Anon

Feed Me!

Part of the challenge is we now live in a continuous loop of feedback. It's incredibly hard to literally switch off to others' opinions. It's everywhere; our appearance, workplace performance, social media, parenting, relationships, career choices, health, fitness, beliefs, values, education, cooking, eating habits, musical tastes, driving . . . it's literally all around us, and more and more we are often encouraged to provide feedback.

To make things even more complicated, feedback can be both wonderful and awful!

I don't know anyone who is entirely comfortable with feedback, unless it's bloody brilliant. And even then, the bloody brilliant feedback can often make so many of us ridiculously uncomfortable!

And let's not forget the joy of receiving contradictory feedback, where one person's 'awesome' is another person's 'meh'. I remember many years ago performing to a sold-out audience at the Fringe Festival here in Edinburgh, and on the same night, for the exact same performance, I got both a five-star and a one-star review.

Wtf?

But that was an important moment for me and my learning. None of us will ever be everyone's cup of tea.

My entire career I have chosen jobs that provide an undeniable platform for judgement.

Primary school teaching . . . kids will be sure to let you know how they feel about you, and as for the parents, don't get me started, especially on the WhatsApp groups, holy shitballs!

Stand-up comedy . . . there is no better feeling than when you have the whole room pissing themselves, eating out the palm of your hand, and no worse feeling than the silence when you don't, that drive home, ooft!

Professional speaker . . . those moments when you move the whole room and set the tone for the whole event are indescribable, as are the moments when the eyes begin to roll. The polite chit chat afterwards, uncomfortable!

Author . . . when someone tells you that your book saved their life, that is, for me, life-enhancing, it makes it all worth it. But when someone hates it and takes to the Amazon review pages to state it publicly, and it's there forever, that hurts.

I get the point of feedback. Of course we can all do better, I understand we can always improve, I accept it's all part of the journey and learning from mistakes is good etc but FFS, in this world of the Joneses, feedback can be shite.

'The best feedback is what we don't want to hear'.

George Raveling

It's such a weird thing. To be told you're a bit shit is, well, shit. To be told you're awesome is great, but on occasion it's awkward. And yet, we're taught that feedback is essential for personal development and growth.

We're told that feedback is great for learning and whether positive *or* negative, it's a positive! So why doesn't it always feel like it?

And even if you do get great feedback then why do so many of us still find the negative? I can have 100 bits of feedback, 99 are lovely but 1 is awful. All I can think about is the 1 and why this person hates me so much?

One moment you're feeling like a rock star, the next your ego is taking a beating. With feedback there's validation, but then there's the valley of despair!

Perhaps it's rooted in our innate desire for improvement, a relentless pursuit of perfection. Or maybe it's a quirk of psychology, where the fear of failure outweighs the joy of success.

During the COVID era I often gave live presentations via the likes of Microsoft Teams. I remember one day my audience was made up of teachers from multiple schools. Some were watching on their own devices, some in their departments and some 2 metres apart in the assembly hall.

'*Remember, feedback is meant to address the problem, not the person*'.

Travis Bradberry

I remember the feedback being generally pretty good. I had tried some new stuff that day, so I was a little nervous, maybe not at my best, likely still figuring out what works online, but overall, the comments that came in were lovely. And then came an email from one secondary teacher in Glasgow. To be clear, this email came in during my presentation . . .

Let me share it with you now. It was titled 'Appalling'. Names of the author and her school have been removed, because I'm not a dick.

Dear Gavin,

I am currently sitting in a school presentation with your organisation. Around me are colleagues shaking their heads in disbelief at the garbage being presented to us. Particularly since this is Friday afternoon before our pupils return on Monday. Plenty more we could be doing.

What an utter load of patronising garbage delivered by an absolute narcissist. Simply pouring out his purile thoughts.

Boring to the point of tears. Utterly pointless for educators. What can we possibly take from this that will enhance our classroom practice?

Appalling

Teacher

Glasgow

As we say here in Scotland, Gaun yersel, Hen!

Just to reiterate, this was sent *during* the presentation. Based on the time it came through, I don't even think I was 30 minutes in. This person was so angry with me that they had to get their phone out and not only tell me, but really *really* fucking tell me!

Like her, you might be wondering what the key themes/takeaways of the presentation were? Please, let me tell you; togetherness, team, glimmers, wellbeing, playfulness, being present, looking for the good stuff around you, being your best self, and kindness . . .

Kindness.

I'll say it again, it was about kindness.

When I first read the email, my anxiety skyrocketed. I think we can all agree that 'tae fuck' is also a wonderful term of measurement, so to put it bluntly, I anxietied tae fuck.

I stared at the email, reading it over and over again trying my absolute hardest to put my finger on what I had done so badly. You see, I am actually quite comfortable with not being everyone's cup of tea, I'm comfortable with ruffling feathers, I have no issues with people not liking my stuff, or challenging other's perceptions and I have had negative feedback on many occasions. I'm human, it happens, I make mistakes, I get it wrong and if there's learning to be had, I take it.

'I am not what you think I am. You are what you think I am'.

Buddha

But *this* email? This email was quite something. It felt personal. Of course it did, I *am* my work. Literally, people pay for Gavin Oattes to speak at their events. That maybe sounds a bit wanky but it's no different from booking a band or a magician or a comedian that you like. I had to learn years ago that because I have wrapped my personality up with my performance, I have to try and not take any criticism of my work as a personal attack.

I have to let it go.

Now, we can try and dissect it, we can put a positive spin on it, find the learning, we can even go down the 'Wow, this individual is clearly miserable, there's obviously other shit going on here' route if we want. Or even the 'this person is a teacher, holy fuck, imagine being a kid in her class?' route, but I can't be bothered.

I thought about replying. My god did I think about replying! I had it *all* written and ready to go, I had to keep telling myself to respond with nothing but kindness and love, but cc the Headteacher in, obvs!

But I never did, it would just consume me. I went from anxiety, to being pissed off, to sadness, to sadness again but for the individual, and then, rightly or wrongly, my team and I had a bit of a chuckle about it. I let go, and we moved on.

It can be tough, but how we receive feedback matters. But there's giving feedback and there's being an absolute fanny.

'The genius of communication is the ability to be totally honest and totally kind at the same time'.

John Powell

How we *give* feedback is where it's at. It's all in the delivery, being the one giving the feedback is tough and it requires thinking, actual prep. Whether it's work related, on social or in person, we have no idea what someone is going through and how our words might make them feel. Feedback and challenge can help or hurt someone.

So, just in case you find yourself in the situation of needing/wanting to give feedback, just ask them! When people feel in control, they're more receptive. Honestly, once they're on board, just explain why you're sharing it, it makes a big difference. Skip the tired 'feedback sandwich', I'm telling you, hiding criticism between fake praise just messes with the message. Remember, empathy! Feedback isn't about fixing someone; it's about understanding their perspective and helping them grow. And most importantly, don't be a dick. No matter your feelings, there's never a need to make it personal.

To wrap up this chapter, here's one of my all-time favourite 'bad' reviews. This was written on Amazon about my book, *Life Will See You Now*. While I fully understand it was meant to be negative, I absolutely adore it and have used it in all my marketing ever since.

Whoever wrote it, you captured the book – and me – perfectly, thank you from the bottom of my heart, I have sold many more books because of you! Perhaps next time you'll be brave enough to put your name against it and I can give you a proper shout out?

Let's give it a nice box . . .

> 'Reads like it's been written by an over enthusiastic teenager who doesn't know how to articulate himself properly'.
>
> *Anon, Amazon*

In a world that demands conformity and where many chase the elusive approval of others, remember, the only opinion that truly defines you is the one you hold of yourself when the world falls silent.

It's only right I mention that social comparison actually isn't all bad, it can give you a burst of pride, a sense of privilege, or even light a fire in your belly to get better. But it can also knock you flat if you're chasing the wrong stuff or trying to measure up to those perfect, airbrushed ideals. The trick is to aim for what genuinely matters, not the glossy nonsense that doesn't.

At the end of the day, it's up to you, there's always a choice.

Decide what kind of life you actually want.

Then say no to everything that isn't that.

CHAPTER 9

Come Back Brighter

ave you ever seen what happens to a young child when they are excited? Everything moves. *Everything*! In fact, it's probably safe to say, they wiggle. And once it starts – if there's enough excitement – the wiggle doesn't stop, the wiggle weaves its way through the whole day like wiggle DNA.

On stage I often chat about when my own kids were tiny and their incredibly uplifting ability to lean into the everyday. The example I often share is from our first family trip abroad, our first foray into the world of 'All inclusive' holidays.

The kids were 7 and 4. Day one, 10:30 a.m. and the kids asked if they could each have an ice-lolly or an ice cream. To be honest I was disappointed in them for not asking sooner!

'Of course you can' I said as I pointed to a giant freezer over beside the bar – the ones that require you to slide the glass open on the top – and told the kids they can go and help themselves.

'Can you give us the money?' Asked my son, Kian.

'You don't need any money, just go and help yourself'. I replied.

Looking at me suspiciously, Kian said 'you can't just help yourself daddy, that's stealing'.

My daughter Ellis piped up, 'We need pennies, Daddy!'

I explained the all-inclusive concept again for the umpteenth time.

'So, we can just go and choose any one we want, and we don't need to pay for it?' Asked Kian.

'Correct'.

'*Any* ice cream Daddy?'

'Yes, *any* ice cream'.

They both looked over at Mummy, she nodded and backed me up with 'that's right guys, what you waiting for?!' Of course, they believed her!

Now, this is where the wiggle happened. Both of them, with every ounce of their wee bodies began to move with excitement, their wee faces lit up, smiles beaming from ear to ear. With everything moving, they wiggled the unstoppable wiggle of excitement.

I have a question for you . . .

When was the last time you were so excited for life, *your* life, that you wiggled? Not just wiggle wiggled, but wiggled the unstoppable wiggle of excitement?

Hold that thought . . .

The kids pirouetted and off they went. Of course, when kids are excited, they can't just walk, they EVERYTHING! Their wee wiggles made up of a sort of dance, run, hop, skip and a jump leaving a trail of smiles around the pool.

They got to the freezer, my son did the honours and slid the top of the freezer open for his wee sister. I must only have turned to my wife for no more than 3 seconds but as I turned back all I could see was two pairs of legs sticking out of the freezer!

My kids were *in* the freezer, fully upside down, swimming in a sea of ice-lolliness. Ice cream Narnia. And I kid you not, they were in there for a long time. Easily 4 minutes.

People were taking photos!

Eventually they popped up, each with two ice-lollies each, a real proud dad moment. They wiggled all the way back to their mum and I, got themselves onto their sunloungers and then for the next 3 or 4 minutes, nothing.

Nothing but silence. Utter contentment. Sheer fulfilment. Present, grateful and fully in the moment.

Onlookers stared.

And what happened next was remarkable. A conversation broke out around the pool among complete strangers from all over the world. The topic of which was something along the lines of *'When was the last time you felt like that?'*

No one could remember . . .

No one.

The first thing I did when we got home, I booked myself in for my first tattoo. And now I have a tattoo of a tiny ice-lolly on my arm. It's small, it's simple and it has a bite taken out of it. While it may be tiny, it's huge in its symbolism and means the world to me. It's a reminder that each and every day I have to notice my glimmers and embrace the sunkick that follows.

It's *my* reminder that the wee things matter.
It's *my* reminder to lean into the ordinary with joy.
It's *my* reminder magic exists in the everyday.
It's *my* reminder not to forget my inner five-year-old.
It's *my* reminder to strive for contentment and fulfilment.
It's *my* reminder to be grateful.
It's *my* reminder to do less and be more.
It's *my* reminder to wiggle.

'We should be able to call in healthy . . . "I'm not coming into the office today, I feel really good and I don't want to waste it on being at work"'.

Anon

Wigglenope

Anyone who's ever been lost knows the grind, the long-haul emotional marathon of clawing your way back to what really matters. It's exhausting, unrelenting and deeply personal, dragging the weight of everything that's happened behind you. Wiggling is definitely not at the forefront of your thoughts!

Part of the problem is that we are just so desperate for everything to be ok again, for life to be great. But that's not how it works, things don't just get better overnight. When you've been so deeply, painfully lost, things take time. Even when you know you're back on the right path and feeling more confident, patience and acceptance are key. There's often another part of the journey to complete; the journey within the journey itself!

After my own 'adventures', I thought I'd feel relief when fear and grief finally loosened their grip. Instead, I was blindsided by something else entirely. I wasn't burned out; my energy had started creeping back. I wasn't depressed, there was now a flicker of hope. But joy? Direction? They were nowhere to be found.

I began to worry this was my new norm, that perhaps the damage was permanent. I hoped it was just another one of the side effects of the antidepressants.

'Sometimes, you don't need to pull yourself together. Sometimes, you just need to sit with your pieces and love them as they are'.

Unknown

I was wigglevoid! Symptoms include sitting still, sighing heavily and an inability to clap along to music. There is – and always should be – room for clapping. There was no clapping.

Had I undergone a wigglectomy? Had there been a wigglepocalypse?

Yes, I had entered wigglevoidium and what I was left with had a name: Wigglenope.

Not really.

I'm told the correct – somewhat more grown-up – terminology is 'Languishing'.

Languishing isn't loud, it's the quiet hum of stagnation and emptiness. It's drifting through days like a ghost, squinting at your life through a smeared, fogged-up windscreen, unsure if you're even at the wheel anymore.

Whilst some go through it on the way down, I hadn't. But it was very much present on the way up.

In the words of writer, Adam Grant, languishing is the neglected middle child of mental health. He describes it as the void between depression and flourishing, the absence of wellbeing. You don't have symptoms of mental illness, but you're not the picture of mental health either.

I'd had my full-blown 'Menty B', I was through the other side but as a result, I wasn't functioning at full capacity, yet. Languishing was messing with my motivation and trashing my ability to focus. I'm told it's more common than major depression, and in some ways it may be a bigger risk factor for mental illness.

The term 'languishing' was coined by sociologist Corey Keyes, who noticed something curious: plenty of people aren't depressed, but they're not exactly thriving either. Keyes' research suggests that the people most at risk for serious depression or anxiety in the next decade aren't the ones battling those symptoms now. It's the ones stuck in the fog of languishing today.

Here's why this matters, languishing is sneaky wee shite. It doesn't do what I did in Melbourne and announce itself with drama or a pipe band. If you're not careful – even on the road to recovery – it can quietly dull your joy, drain your drive and let you lose your wee piece of magic.

The journey back is never straightforward, full of ups and downs, you will have moments where you don't even realise you're sliding, your spark will fade again but it will be so gradual, it feels normal. And when you don't see the problem and catch it early, you're not likely to fix it. Remember, patience and acceptance are key.

'Your present circumstances don't determine where you can go; they merely determine where you start'.

Nido Qubein

Even if you're not in this fog yourself, chances are you know someone who is. Recognising it is the first step towards helping them (and maybe yourself) rekindle a little light, and possibly even getting their wiggle back!

This isn't just in your head, it's in the air we breathe, the culture we're steeped in. You can't slap a sticking plaster on a world that's fundamentally out of tune and expect it to heal. We live in a society that openly rallies around broken bodies but still whispers behind closed doors about broken minds. Physical health? Totally normalised. Mental health? Still a stigma fest. Still a shitshow.

It's time for a reset. Time to stop pretending that 'not depressed' means you're thriving or that 'not burned out' equals bursting with energy. Because the truth is, there's fucking millions of us stuck in a weird in-between, surviving but not exactly living.

Languishing. That's the word. A quiet ache, a foggy void. But naming it? That's the first step to shaking it. By acknowledging this collective 'meh' we're wading through, we give it less power.

It's time to stop settling for *'fine'* and start daring to aim for *'alive'*. It takes serious effort. Dig deep, friends. Let's not just acknowledge the struggle, let's light the path forward, together.

Every moment is meant move on . . .

Day One Beats One Day

Have you ever caught yourself saying, 'One day I'll do that' or 'I'll start tomorrow'? Sound familiar? We all do it. But here's a little secret, 'One day' rarely comes. What if we flipped that around and made today your Day One? You know that day when you stop waiting and start doing.

'Day One' means you're making moves. It's when you decide to stop putting things off and go for it. Whether it's learning a new skill, trying something that scares you, setting a goal or choosing to rediscover your wiggle, 'Day One' is about making the choice to start.

'To begin, begin'.

William Wordsworth

I mentioned 'Flow' in Chapter 3. Interestingly, new challenges, meaningful work and experiences that spark something in you, those are solid ways to shake off languishing. But let's not sugarcoat it, if your focus is shot, flow isn't going to happen. You can't lose yourself in the moment if your mind keeps pulling you somewhere else.

I found that actually carving out daily time to focus on some sort of challenge that matters to me works, my list of every brilliant thing, writing, cooking, meaningful conversation. Sometimes this stuff was a small step towards rediscovering some of the energy and enthusiasm I'd missed during all those months.

The truth is, sometimes life feels like a series of challenges. But with the right mindset, every challenge becomes an opportunity. When you choose to look at life like that, even the tough stuff can turn into something awesome. Positivity and mindset are like your secret weapons. They won't make everything easy, but they can help you stay strong, keep going and maybe even have a little fun along the way.

From the fabulous *Ratatouille*

Django: The world we live in belongs to the enemy. We must live carefully. We look out for our own kind, Remy. When all is said and done, we're all we've got.

Remy: No.

Django: [*turning back*] What?

Remy: No. Dad, I don't believe it. You're telling me, that the future is – can '*only*' be – more of '*this*'?

Django: This is the way things are. You can't change nature.

Remy: Change *is* nature, Dad. The part that *we* can influence. And it starts when we decide. [*turns to leave*]

Django: Where are you going?

Remy: With luck, forward.

Life is full of moments where we hesitate, worrying about what might go wrong or how hard something might be. But we're told from a young age, challenges aren't roadblocks, they're stepping stones. They're how we grow. Sure, things will be shit sometimes, but instead of saying 'One day', why not decide, 'Today is day one'?

You can choose 'Day One' without being cheerful all the time, that's not what positivity is about. It's about embracing challenges with an open mind and a 'let's do this' attitude. Instead of seeing difficulties as problems, try seeing them as chances to get better, stronger or smarter.

In the moments you know exactly what you should be doing, stop looking for other things to do, stop being a 'puterofferer' and put the trolley away.

You don't actually need this book, or another podcast, or another course. Instead, figure out why you aren't doing the things you know you should be.

Start today. However small. And while you will make mistakes from time to time, day one always beats one day.

The Upside of Oops

Take a moment to think about the best stories you've ever heard. Do they start with, 'I planned everything perfectly, and it all went exactly as expected'? Of course not. They begin with a fuck up, a blunder or some gloriously cringeworthy moment.

Mistakes are a fact of life. Essential even. We tell people it's okay to mess up, but what about when it's *us* making the mistakes? We're never going to get everything right, and deep down, we know this. So why does it feel so terrible? Why do we hold ourselves to such impossibly high standards when, in truth, messing up is how we learn, and sometimes, it makes for the best stories.

Take, for example, one of the funniest mistakes I've ever come across: the 'Penis Island' translation blunder. A great friend of mine, Eddie, brought this to my attention as he captured the joyful moment in a video of his dad recounting the story. In Scotland, there's been a wonderful push to include

Gaelic translations on street and landmark signs. Admirable in theory, but as with all big projects, there have been some missteps.

One particularly memorable sign on the Isle of Bute – an idyllic island off Scotland's west coast – was meant to welcome visitors with the phrase, 'Welcome to the beauty of the Isle of Bute'. A lovely sentiment, except that for nearly *nine years,* the Gaelic translation on the sign read, 'Welcome to the beauty of Penis Island'. Let that sink in!

Imagine the gift shop . . .

Eddie's dad, reading this out loud between fits of uncontrollable laughter, could barely get the words out. The video of him giggling so hard has become my go-to whenever I need cheering up. It's not just the absurdity of the mistake; it's the sheer joy in Eddie's dad's laughter that makes it so utterly infectious.

Moments like this remind us of the upside of fucking up. Mistakes can feel mortifying in the moment, but they're often the source of our greatest stories and biggest laughs. We stumble, we fall, and sometimes, we land on something unexpectedly wonderful. As poet Darby Hudson so beautifully put it, there's an inherent positivity with the word 'up' in 'fuck *up*', you're not falling down, it's not down or sideways, you're flying.

'If you're not making mistakes, you're not doing anything interesting'.

Billie Joe Armstrong

Sure, mistakes can feel terrible at first. We worry about what others might think, and the weight of self-imposed perfectionism drags us down. But when we allow ourselves to laugh – even just a little – we create space for healing and growth. Laughter transforms frustration into lightness and regret into joy.

Fucking up is inevitable, I still remember revealing a Scottish premiership football team's new shirt on social media before it had been officially launched. Literally, no fans or media had seen it yet and here's me, a non-football fan posting pics of it. No-one actually knows about this, not even my best friends. It's so ridiculous, I could be making the whole thing up, but I'm not. I still don't really understand exactly how it even happened, but the phone call that day, direct from the club director, who was literally on the bus with the players, on the way to a match haunts me. I lost sleep over that one.

And then there's the time I think I was kidnapped!

But seriously. It was 2001, and I was fresh-faced, naive and armed with the misplaced confidence of someone who hadn't watched enough documentaries about bad decisions abroad.

My friend Rory and I had just landed in Bangkok, wide-eyed and eager. After demolishing what I still maintain was the greatest meal of my life, we asked the hotel manager where we could grab a beer. A simple beer. Nothing fancy. Just a cold one nearby.

The manager, clearly sensing our 'just-off-the-plane' energy, said he'd arrange a *limo* for us. Now, this wasn't a stretch Hummer or anything, in Bangkok, they call any taxi a limo. We should've seen this as our first clue that things weren't going to go as planned.

Minutes later, Rory and I were in the backseat of a rickety taxi, engaging in a hilariously unproductive conversation with the driver:

Driver: Where you wanna go?

Me: Bar.

Driver: You wanna *chow*?

Me: No food, thank you. Beer!

Driver: You wanna *smoke*?

Me: Nope! Just beer!

Driver: You wanna see show?

It was at this point the penny dropped, by 'show', he meant a *show-show*. The kind of show you probably wouldn't want to explain to your parents.

'Absolutely not', I said, 'No show. Just beer'.

And that's when it happened.

The driver locked the doors. And floored it.

Rory and I exchanged a look. The kind of look that says, 'This is how people end up on the news'.

The taxi shot down the road like it was auditioning for *The Fast and the Furious*, a sharp right turn, we found ourselves rattling down the narrowest alleyway I've ever seen. The cobblestones beneath the tyres made the whole car shake.

The walls of the alley got closer and closer. Another turn, another jolt and then – screech – the car came to a sudden halt.

Outside a laundrette.

In a dark, desolate alleyway. In Bangkok.

Two giant men appeared out of the shadows like they'd been summoned by some dodgy ritual. They opened the car doors and gestured for us to get out. At this point, I was 90% sure we were about to be sold for spare organs.

The driver sped off without a word, leaving Rory and me standing there, utterly bewildered, in a scene that felt like the opening of a bad action movie.

One of the men opened the door to the laundrette and gestured for us to go inside.

Inside? Into the creepiest laundrette of all time?

The place was abandoned. No lights. Rusty machines that probably hadn't spun a sock since the 1980s. Rory, in his infinite wisdom, leaned over and whispered, 'We need to just go with it'.

Spoiler: we should NOT have gone with it.

One of the men held out his hand and said, 'Baht'. Of course, baht is the local currency. At this point, I was convinced we'd stumbled into some underground drug operation. I vividly remember thinking, *What would Bruce Willis do?*

'Two things are infinite: the universe and human stupidity; and I'm not sure about the universe'.

Albert Einstein

We handed over what little baht we had, because what choice did we have? I was certain we were about to get tumble-dried to death.

We handed over the cash. And that's when it got worse.

The blokes led us through the laundrette, down a narrow corridor, and into the back of a nightclub. I say 'nightclub', but honestly, it felt more like the waiting room for hell. The place was packed with Westerners, every single one of them wearing the same expression: a mix of horror and fascination.

On stage? The most degrading scenes I've ever seen in my life. I'm not gonna describe it here, because frankly, I'm trying to forget it. Let's just say it made me want to shower in bleach.

Rory and I exchanged a look that said, We need to leave. *Now!*

But there was no obvious way out. I started to panic, thinking, *This is it. My life's going to end here, surrounded by sadness and ping-pong balls.*

We spotted a door marked 'Exit'. We bolted for it, pushing past confused tourists and avoiding the glare of enormous staff.

The second we hit the street, we didn't stop. We ran like our arses were on fire.

Then, out of nowhere, we saw salvation: a tuk-tuk. It looked like a thatched cottage on three wheels, held together with duct tape and hope. We jumped in, shouting, 'Drive! Just drive!'

The driver didn't even ask questions. He took off, weaving through stray cats and dogs as we clung on for dear life. And there we were, two traumatised lads from Troon rattling through the streets of Bangkok, wondering what the hell had just happened.

Now I kind of laugh about it. Not what we saw but rather the absolute ridiculousness of it all. We were on a layover. One night in Bangkok. We just wanted a beer. At no point did we think we would live out our own awful movie from the late 1980s.

There are glimmers in our missteps, and we don't just learn from them. Sometimes, they're where the magic happens, and with a little humour and perspective, fucking up is also an invitation to embrace life's imperfections, to let go of shame, and to find beauty . . . even on Penis Island.

The Great Resilience Buzz

Everyone is talking about resilience these days. They have been for years, but still, every event I am booked to speak at, resilience is forever a key theme. I'd maybe go as far to say we're obsessed with it but sometimes I wonder if people actually know what it is, or how to define it?

'If at first you don't succeed, then skydiving definitely isn't for you'.

Steven Wright

It's how we come back from being down, how we recover from failure, knockbacks, losing. So many refer to it as 'bouncebackability', such a shit word. From this day forward, I propose we rebrand the word resilience as 'reboundaciousness'.

Or 'rolypolyforwardability'.

I sometimes struggle with it too, in both the understanding *and* the doing. The experts tell us it's a 'foundational psychological tool that empowers us to feel effective and capable of handling uncertainty'.

But despite this, I'm not really sure exactly what it is? Is it a quality, skill or personality trait? Is it genetically determined or is it taught?

One thing I know for sure is that we can get better at it! Experts confirm that resilience is a quality *and* a skill, that with effort and consistency, can be enhanced.

Another thing I know for sure is we're not jellyfish, fact. Specifically, we're not Turritopsis Dohrnii, the biologically immortal jellyfish that can hit a cosmic reset button and revert to its baby form whenever things get tough. Imagine the luxury! Missed a deadline? Bam, back to day one. Said something awkward at a party? Abracadabra, tiny jelly again.

Unfortunately, we don't have that superpower. We can't just 'start over'. Life doesn't let us reboot; it nudges (or shoves) us forward. Resilience, then, isn't about erasing the hard stuff. It's about pushing through it, scratched, bruised and all.

'We're more than just our yesterday'.

Eddie Vedder

But here's where our jellyfish friends have inspired me! While we can't rewind time, we *can* take mini-resets. Since my life was turned upside down, when I feel like my physical, emotional or mental batteries are about to short-circuit, I stop and ask, 'What does a reset look like right now?' Sometimes, it's as simple as a 10-minute walk, a deep breath or abandoning my to-do list to watch an episode of 'A Place in the Sun' (such a good show!). These micro-resets don't erase the challenges, it's not an escape, but they recharge my ability to face them head-on.

So no, we're not jellyfish, we're human. We grow and we endure. And instead of restarting, we rewrite our story as we push forward.

But, as some of us know all too well, 'reboundaciousness' is such a personal journey. With a need for small, incremental wins along the way, it's our habits that form the foundation of our mental beliefs that matter when the going gets tough.

Purpose Built

Positive psychology teaches us that finding meaning in our work/ environment/life is right up there on the list of 'must-haves' when it comes to building resilience.

'Everything can be taken from a man but one thing: the last of his human freedoms – to choose one's attitude in any given set of circumstances. To choose one's way'.

Viktor Frankl

Psychologists keep finding the same thing, having a strong sense of purpose isn't just nice, it's a game-changer. It helps you roly-poly forward when life's kicking your ass, boosts mental sharpness and keeps you grounded. But purpose doesn't just make you feel good, it protects your brain from the damage stress can cause. To paraphrase Dr Patricia Doyle, a neuropsychologist with the Alzheimer Disease Centre, having a sense of purpose might be one of the best things you can do for your brain.

'Purpose somehow gives your brain resilience. It makes your brain stronger and more resistant to the effects of diseases like Alzheimer's'.

Boyle

Other scientific studies support that having a strong purpose directly correlates with how well and how long we're going to live. Recent research suggests that finding meaning in life's experiences, especially when facing challenges, is a key mechanism of resilience.

Robert Butler along with the National Institute of Health researched health and longevity and reported findings in his book *'Why Survive? Being Old in America'*. Get this, people who had a strong sense of purpose lived longer than those who didn't have a clear purpose!

Dan Buettner, who founded Blue Zones, has also done worldwide research around this stuff. In studying women of Okinawa, Japan, it was discovered that one of the key reasons for their longevity is their strong sense of purpose.

I think it's fair to say there's a pattern forming here!

Not everyone lies awake at night craving a grand philosophy of life or a carefully polished 'why'. But let's face it: mattering matters. Purpose isn't just a fluffy add-on, it's the secret sauce to being human. Knowing you make a difference? That's what keeps the wheels turning. As we level up in life – wrestling with the psychological, the emotional and maybe even the spiritual – that itch for meaning starts to scratch harder. At some point, we hit a crossroads, stuck in the mud, wondering if our wheels are just spinning on the spot. 'Is this it? What's the point? Is this all we are?' It's the big questions that smack you in the face when the old routines stop cutting it.

Years ago, someone told me I was an 'experiment of one'. I love this. And so are you! No one else has your blueprint, so why follow their rules? You're a walking, talking hypothesis of gallusness, of awesomeness, designed to evolve. Designed to experiment boldly!

'Find out who you are and do it on purpose . . . preferably without scaring everyone around you'.

Dolly Parton

Legendary coach and author Richard Leider tells us that our purpose isn't something we just 'get'. Yes, it does require some work, but the search for life purpose is far more straight-forward than we might expect. Some books out there would have us believe it's something mystical or mysterious, it's simply not.

It's natural to seek meaning in our lives. It's rarely revealed to us without some digging, and getting it wrong, over and over, is part of the process. It's how we grow. It's how we human!

Grab a cuppa, take 15 minutes for yourself and answer the following questions:

Purpose Reflection Activity

1. Why are you? (weird question, I know)
2. Why do you get up in the morning?
3. What keeps you awake at night?
4. When are you most alive?
5. What does being successful mean to you?
6. How might you apply your gifts to a pursuit that is of deep interest to you and helps others?

7. What can you do to make a difference in one person's life, today?
8. What is your sentence? (Another weird one, if you summarised your purpose in one short sentence, what would it be?)
9. If you say yes to living purposefully, what do you say no to?
10. If you met an older version of yourself, what sage advice would they give you?

Look back at what you've written. Embrace your answers as a signpost, not a destination, like GPS breadcrumbs leading you to your best self! Think of them as clues to who you are and what you care about most.

'People who really want to make a difference in the world usually do it, in one way or another. And I've noticed something about people who make a difference in the world: they hold the unshakable conviction that individuals are extremely important, that every life matters'.

Beth Clarke

One key thing I've learned is that purpose evolves, it grows and develops with us through the different phases of life. A progressive unlocking of purpose is essential to our health, happiness and longevity.

Live deliberately, collect your glimmers, show them off, leave a trail of pebbles and *always* leave things a little brighter than how you found them.

Pebbles, Gav?

Yeah, you know, the quiet wee plops? Ok, not sure that sounds right . . .

Let's call it *Pebble Theory* . . . sounds like a Coldplay B-side or a mindfulness app.

Here's how it works: Every small act you drop into the world, every smile, text, coffee bought, daft joke told, compliment given, moment held, is a pebble. And pebbles cause ripples.

Ripples travel. They touch people you'll never meet. They change moods, minds, days.

Some bounce off. Some vanish.

But now and then, one lands just right and changes *everything*.

So, the next time you think 'what difference will it make?', remember this: the Grand Canyon wasn't carved by one big event.

It was a billion tiny droplets showing up every day and doing their thing.

And then came the penguins.

Now, I know what you're thinking.

'Gav, mate . . . what the hell do penguins have to do with pebbles?'

EVERYTHING.

'Sometimes when I consider what tremendous consequences come from little things . . . I am tempted to think there are no little things'.

Bruce Barton

Let me take you to the icy shores of Antarctica, where the most romantic creatures in the world live, the Adélie penguins. See, when a male penguin falls for a female, he doesn't buy her roses or write her a sonnet or send her a flirty DM.

He finds her a pebble.

Not just any pebble, the *perfect* pebble. Smooth. Shiny. Full of promise.

He waddles over, presents it at her feet, and waits. If she likes it, she adds it to her nest. If she really likes *him*, they shack up and raise baby penguins together.

That's it. That's the courtship.

A pebble.

It's not about the rock. It's about the gesture. The effort. The 'I chose this just for you' of it all.

And that, my friends, is pure fire-in-the-belly stuff.

So yes, channel your inner penguin.

Show up with your pebble, a kind word, a moment of realness, a bloody good hug, and chuck it down like it matters.

Because it *does*.

I'm not saying don't dream big. Dream huge. Dream ridiculous. But live small, beautiful, intentional moments along the way. Every laugh, every nudge, every little check-in is a ripple. And enough ripples? That's a wave. Enough waves? That's a fucking tsunami.

So here's your mission, should you choose to accept it: Pebbling.

Drop one pebble a day. A call. A compliment. A dance. A smile you mean.

And if you're feeling confident . . .

Drop a pebble where it's least expected. The grumpy guy at work. The old school pal you haven't messaged in years. The bus driver who always looks knackered.

Go full penguin on them. Plop with pride . . . PEBBLE with pride.

Let's Do This!

Life is bursting with lovely, heart-warming moments. Well, sometimes it is. Let's not pretend though, it can also be full on, terrifying and at times proper scary!

Let me tell about one of the scariest moments of my entire life. 16 April 2011, I arrived home from work to find my wife in labour. Don't worry, that's not the scary part, I knew she was pregnant.

The pangs had only just begun 2 minutes before I walked through the door. This would be our second child and with our first child taking 25 hours to appear, I figured I had a few hours at least.

I called the hospital to give them the update and they routinely told me to keep an eye on her and update them if anything changes or speeds up.

Just as I hung up the phone my wife's waters broke. I picked the phone right back up, called the hospital and again they told me to hang fire and keep an eye on things.

Not a chance.

Instead, I bundled Ali (carefully) into the car, handed her a mars bar (crucial advice right there), grabbed the Digestives (more important advice) and headed for the hospital.

Of course, it had to be 5:35 p.m. on a Wednesday evening. In Edinburgh city centre.

Edinburgh traffic doesn't move particularly fast at the best of times but in peak time with many a cyclist and a few trams thrown in for good measure, it is particularly slow. Add to this the potential arrival of an Oattes child, we have a moment never to be forgotten.

It was now 5:45 p.m. and we were literally at a standstill. Ali was doing what all women do; being awesome. I was doing what all men do, shitting myself.

On a scale of 1–10 for shitting oneself, I had shat to 11.

'I CAN FEEL THE HEAD' screamed Ali.

My world at this point seemed to go into slow motion.

My thought process went as follows . . .

1. Can I deliver a baby?
2. Yes.

Already you can probably sense I wasn't thinking 100% clearly. In my mind I was now a midwife.

In the back of the car we had a towel and some water, how hard can it be . . . right?

'THE BABY'S COMING NOW' screamed Ali.

Just at this moment I saw a large police van driving towards us. I leapt out the car and stood right in the way of it. I waved my hands, and they stopped.

The male officer who was in the driving seat asked me what was wrong.

'My wife is in the car and she's having a baby right now!'

He sighed and rolled his eyes. Literally, I couldn't believe it!

My world at this point seemed to go into slow motion once again.

My thought process went as follows . . .

1. Did he just sigh and roll his eyes?
2. Yes he did, but I'm a midwife, it's fine.

Again, not thinking particularly clearly . . .

All of a sudden, the female officer in the passenger seat leant over and asked *'What did you just say?'*

I replied, *'My wife is having an actual baby right now!'*

Then came my favourite bit.

With the back of her hand, she smacked the male officer across the chest, put both hands in the air and yelled 'LET'S DO THIS!'

What followed next was all a bit of a blur, but there were blue lights, sirens and a traffic jam that parted like the Red Sea.

'Some people walk into the fire. Others dance in it'.

Unknown

With a police escort we arrived just in the nick of time and by 6:03 p.m. my daughter Ellis arrived like a bullet from a gun.

What I learned in this moment is that there are two types of people when faced with a terrifying or stressful situation. We met both that day.

There's Keith, our male officer. And there's Hilary, our female officer.

Keith rolled his eyes. I'm sure he is a lovely man, but he rolled his eyes. An actual baby was coming into the actual world and he rolled his actual eyes.

Hilary punched the air with two hands and shouted, 'let's do this!'.

All through life we meet Keiths, and we meet Hilarys. In every situation life throws at us we get to make a choice in the moment.

Sometimes it's hard.

Sometimes it's terrifying.

But I choose never to roll my eyes.

I choose Hilary.

Be more Hilary.

That Was a Lot!
(Shout Out to Me)

Y ou're on your own, kid, you always have been. But you're not alone.

Gav, did you just use another Taylor Swift lyric?

Yeah, I definitely did. And it cuts straight to the heart of things.

So I'll say it again . . .

You're on your own, kid, you always have been. But you're not alone.

I think Taylor is reminding us that, for better or worse, this is *your* journey. There's something starkly beautiful about that truth. Her words are not meant to break you, they're meant to remind you of your own strength. You've weathered every storm so far. You've stood up, over and over, when the world knocked you down. That's strength. That's reboundaciousness. That's you.

But, 'You're not alone' matters here. Sure, you're the headliner, that means you get to call the shots and take the credit. But every headliner needs a great roadie, a great sound engineer, a band perhaps. And then there's your audience, holding up a lighter just for you, signing the fuck out of your song!

Nobody was built to carry it all. You're not meant to do it all by yourself.

'Just because no one else can heal or do your inner work for you doesn't mean you can, should or need to do it alone'.

Lisa Olivera

Even on the hardest days, when sadness seems to be riding shotgun, you're not alone. Look up, there's always someone cheering you on. Sometimes they're loud and obvious. Other times, it's quieter, a smile from a stranger, a song lyric that hits you right in the soul or even a memory. A glimmer.

Never forget, the world's got your back more than you know.

Boys Get Sad Too

As I sit writing this final chapter, I feel a curious mix of emotions. I'm hopeful, apprehensive, maybe a wee bit proud. Just hours ago, I returned from the doctor with news to share, we have a plan to begin the transition away from antidepressants. A long-term plan. Zero rush. I had no goal to come off them, they have been a real positive for me, they work, but it's the culmination of a journey that has tested me in every possible way, yet one that has also revealed my capacity for resilience and growth. It kinda feels like a full circle moment, that has absolutely, most definitely *not* been a circle. More a rhombicosidodecahedron.

A what?

A rhombicosidodecahedron.

Even saying it is exhausting.

Yeah, this is my full rhombicosidodecahedron moment. 20 triangular faces, 30 square faces, 12 pentagonal faces, 60 vertices and 120 edges. And I covered them all. Twice.

A mental health day that lasted over 20 months. 20 months. That's how long I've spent looking for the fragments of myself I feared – certainly at one stage – were lost forever. Searching for joy amid chaos. Navigating grief, doubt and anxiety. Seeking meaning, exploring new paths, hunting for the smallest glimmers of light in the dark. Scouring my past, my habits, my very soul to rediscover what truly matters. And now, standing on the other side, I can say this with certainty, I have found it.

I have found *me*.

And guess what, Taylor Swift? I am not the problem.

It's not me.

But I am the part of the solution.

'I'm not the person I was yesterday. I'm always becoming'.

David Bowie

Found, in the 'Lost and Found'. Not the person I once was, but maybe someone stronger, maybe more whole and definitely more attuned to life's quiet beauty. For too long, I let what happened to me and my family eat me up, weigh me down and fill me with fear. But now, I accept it. I accept how it has shaped me, how it has broken and rebuilt me in ways I never imagined.

I didn't ask for it to happen, but I learned how cruel life can be and how quickly it can all change. I learned how just one minute can spark an entire joy sabbatical.

I learned one minute can change a life.

I'm not fixed. But I feel a lot less broken. No one tells you how hard it is to rewire your brain to allow amazing things to happen again after so much trauma or pain. This is not the end of my story. There's more to come, and I will anxiety another day, of that I am sure. I might once again need medical help, and I will definitely – through choice – see my therapist again. I cannot tell you just how comfortable I am with this.

But this feels like the start of something new, a life lived with more purpose, more clarity, and a profound gratitude for both the struggles and the triumphs that have brought me here.

And in becoming a better version of myself, I give the best of me to those around me. That's the beauty of having a purpose, it's never just about you. It's about the ripples you create when you show up with intention. It's in how you make things brighter, how you leave things better, the mark you leave behind. Purpose isn't in the taking; it's in the giving. It's the energy you pour into the world that sparks something extraordinary in others. And when you do that, when you truly lean into what lights you up, joy finds its way back to you, filling you up, effortlessly.

So ask yourself, what the bloody hell are you gonna do with this one wild, magical, terrifying, unpredictable, beautiful, tragically short wee life of yours?

What – from the bottom of your heart – the fuck do you want?

Optimist Prime

It's difficult, we're not exactly living in the age of optimism, are we? I think we can all agree on one thing, optimism feels like it's gone AWOL. We're living in an age where doomscrolling is practically a sport, and the news is like a 24/7, all-inclusive buffet of bleak. Journalist Dylan Matthews nailed it back in 2023, our media's negativity bias isn't just a passing mood, it's a full-blown obsession. And guess what? It's only getting worse.

We're wired to zoom in on the blips, the bad news, the spikes in crime, war or chaos. Long-term progress over the past decades is rarely acknowledged. Positive trends? Sorry, not clickbait-worthy. Instead, we're laser-focused on what's broken, what's flawed and what's failed.

But it doesn't stop there. We've even managed to turn *good news* into *bad news*. It's as if we're allergic to celebrating wins, always needing to add a pinch of pessimism to the mix. 'Hey, look! This amazing thing happened!' quickly turns into, 'Yeah, but let's not get carried away. It could still go wrong'.

Negativity is contagious, and it's messing with our heads. Some of us are so tuned into what's wrong that we forget to notice what's right. But what if we flipped it? What if, instead of staring at the cracks in the pavement, we lifted our heads and looked at the sky?

'You're always a montage away from being a boxer'.

Anon

Ash Buchanan is one of my heroes in the world of mindset. His stuff is magic, be sure to check him out. One of the many things he writes about is mindset shifts, and my goodness does the world need a mindset shift, preferably towards optimism!

Ash teaches us that mindset shifts are natural processes likening them to arising and unfolding in much the same way as a caterpillar naturally transforms into a butterfly.

You'd be forgiven for thinking of mindset shifts as the dog's bollocks of personal growth, those moments when you see the world differently, and everything clicks into place. But not all mindset shifts are created equal. Some bubble up naturally, some are yanked into place by sheer force, and others? Well, they get stuck in the queue, waiting for a green light that never comes.

The Surprise Party for Your Soul

Let's start with the good stuff, what Buchanan calls organic shifts. These are the moments that catch you off guard, like when you're in the middle of a walk, lost in thought, and suddenly – BAM! – you see life like you're five again. It's glimmer central! It's like your brain has been sneaking a peek at a more awesome version of you and decided, 'Hey, let's call in for that person and see if they're coming out to play'.

Organic shifts happen when we're truly present, living in the *now*. They're not planned, and they're certainly not controlled. They just *are*. They align with your essence, your core, the stuff that makes you *you*. It's beautiful, it's real, and it feels like coming home. Interestingly though you've got to slow down enough to let them happen.

The Puppet Show

Then there are the controlled shifts, the ones that feel a bit like a puppet show. There's a plan, a strategy, and someone – maybe you, maybe someone else – is pulling the strings. These shifts can still get you where you need to go, but they're more about the destination than the journey.

Controlled shifts aren't bad; they're just, well, controlled. Goal setting, strategic planning, all those buzzwords we love in self-help land, they work, but they also come with a cost. They can shit all over the magic of those organic, unexpected moments. It's like painting by numbers instead of letting your creativity run wild. Sure, you'll end up with a picture, but will it really be *your* masterpiece?

The Snooze Button of Life

And then, there's the sad tale of the postponed shift, the one that should've happened but didn't. Why? Because we're clinging to old mindsets like a favourite pair of shoes, even though they're worn out and don't really feel the way they used to. Or maybe it's deeper than that, maybe there's trauma, fear, or hurt holding us back, leaving us stuck.

'You need to learn to select your thoughts just the same way you select your clothes every day. This is a superpower you can cultivate. If you want to control things in your life . . . work on the mind'.

Elizabeth Gilbert

Keep in mind, those postponed shifts are *ready*. They're tapping on the window, asking to be let in. They're ready for you to come out and play. But the longer you avoid them, the more they pile up, and before you know it, they're in the Dead Letters Office.

Control Freaks Unite

We're masters of the controlled shift. We love a good plan. We adore a solid goal. And hey, there's nothing wrong with a bit of direction, except when it drowns out the possibility of something more organic, more spontaneous, more *alive*.

We've got to ask ourselves: are we so busy strategising our mindset shifts that we're missing the moments that could naturally lead us there? Are we so hung up on control that we're forgetting how to let go?

The Shift to Optimism

So what's the way forward? It's not about ditching control entirely, it's about creating space for the organic. It's about recognising when we're clinging to the old mindsets and gently letting them go. And yes, it's about healing the traumas that hold us back, so we can finally step into the shifts that have been waiting for us all along.

Imagine a world where we embraced a mindset of optimism, not as a cheesy platitude, but as a real, grounded, intentional shift. A world where we balanced planning with presence, control with curiosity and strategy with spontaneity.

'I hate when people make fun of me for being positive and spreading good vibes like fuck your bitter ass, I spent a good portion of my life being bitter sad and angry so if I wanna shoot sunshine out my ass then I fuckin will'.

Anon

Embracing optimism doesn't make us immune to stress and worries. Life will still smack you in the face with all its might. But optimism isn't a daft wee trick, it teaches us how to see what is going wrong and still be hopeful that it can be turned right. As a positive psychology intervention, optimism partly helps in building resilience, teaches us radical acceptance and motivates in the form of hope to keep going.

Optimism also isn't about ignoring the bad stuff; it's about shining a light on the good and accepting the bad. It's about choosing to believe that progress is happening, even if it's messy and imperfect. It's about refusing to let the bad news drown out the good. And, as if it needs any more selling, optimism is directly associated with *reduced* depression, anxiety and stress.

That's the shift we need. We can *all* learn to be more optimistic. The world needs it. And if you want, it starts now.

Inspired by *New York Times* bestselling author, Mark Murphy, here's a lovely wee exercise to increase your optimism quickly if you're willing to honestly assess the people in your life . . .

Step 1: Sussing the Usual Suspects

Right, think about the 10 people who hog most of your time. You know who I mean. It could be your family, your friends, your work pals or that one guy across the road who always wants to chat about Brexit (FFS) while you're trying to clean your car.

Have a wee nosey through your phone calls, FaceTime, Zoom/Teams meetings, and whatever else you've been up to. The idea is to figure out who's got the lead roles in your life. Please note, 10 is not a magic number, you can do 5, 15, however many you like. The important thing is to narrow it down so you can see what's what. Or who's what . . .

Step 2: Rate Their Outlook

This is where it gets interesting. Take your list and rate each person from −10 (the kind of pessimist who makes Eeyore look like sunshine) to +10 (someone so cheery it's annoying). As Murphy points out, this sounds a bit cold and calculating but bear in mind that you're not passing judgement on a person's value or worth, you're merely assessing their optimism or pessimism. Effectively we're figuring out who's got the sunny vibes and who's dragging around their own personal rain cloud.

I have close friends/family that are incredibly optimistic while others are severely pessimistic. And I have those who truly believe they are positive, yet they can talk about nothing but problems. It doesn't make one friend better than another; it just makes them different.

'You are the books you read, the films you watch, the music you listen to, the people you spend time with, the conversation you engage in. Choose wisely what you feed your mind'.

Jac Vanek

Step 3: Chase the Sunshine

Here's the plan: once you've got your ratings sorted, make an effort to spend more time with the optimistic lot. If Louise is an eight and Chris is a nine, then FFS, go hang out with them! Call them up, go for a walk or just stick them on a video call to brighten your day. Surround yourself with their good energy, it's like borrowing someone else's central heating when your boiler's knackered.

Now, I'm not saying you should boot the pessimists out of your life entirely. That'd be cruel, especially if someone's struggling. But you've got to protect your own headspace. If you've just spent 40 minutes on the phone with someone who's convinced the sky's falling, balance it out by chatting with someone who can make you laugh till your sides hurt. It's not about ditching people; it's about keeping *yourself* in decent emotional shape.

The Grand Plan

It's really simple:

1. **Be honest** about who's taking up your time.
2. **Do something about it** and shift your focus to the people who lift you up.

And ignore the ones who roll their eyes at the idea of optimism! This isn't happy clappy nonsense; this is damn good for you, in fact, it's life enhancing. Remember, it takes a bit of effort, and it may even require some difficult decisions e.g. backing off from family can be tough, trust me, I know. But the payoff is absolutely massive.

There is technically a number 3, the flipside to this, which is to consider just what type of friend/colleague you yourself are! What list would you be on? Are *you* a good friend? We rarely stop to ask this about ourselves, many of us are too busy picking faults in others! I reckon most people *think* they are, but when you start to really think about it, I question whether most of us are in fact *really* good friends.

I've recently been questioning my own levels of 'being a *great* friend' and my own optimism around others. I fully accept I have work to do, there are some improvements needed.

Ask yourself this; when was the last time you put the effort in and did the hard work for your friends? Your colleagues? Your partner?

Make today day one . . .

What Really Matters?

Deep in the depths of the Amazon rainforest, there's something going on, and even the experts are baffled. The Tsimanes (Chee-ma-neys), a semi-nomadic indigenous community that has apparently cracked the code for staying young, fit and gloriously alive. These folks don't just dabble in life; they grab it with both hands and hang on tight.

Picture this: 84-year-old Martina Canchi Nate, out there in the jungle, digging up yucca roots and chopping plantains like a pro. She's not thinking about retiring or days spent in a recliner, this is optimism personified, this is life lived!

And it's not just Martina. For the Tsimanes, her vitality is the rule, not the exception. Numbering around 16,000 strong, this Bolivian tribe has scientists scratching their heads and questioning their own gym memberships. Why? Because the Tsimanes have the healthiest arteries on the planet. No, seriously. These people are out here ageing slower than the rest of us. Their brains? Practically ageless. Alzheimer's? Barely even heard of it.

So, what's the secret? It's not in a lab or a luxury retreat. It's in the way they live, raw, real, optimistic and ridiculously in tune with nature. Their lives are a symphony of movement. While most of us are glued to screens and stuck in chairs, they're out there hunting, gathering, weaving roofs and growing their own food. Their diet? Forget processed junk or sugar overloads; it's pure, unfiltered, straight-from-the-earth goodness. Think fibre-packed roots, fruit, fresh game and meals smoked on an open fire.

A 75-year-old Tsimane has arteries that would make your average 50-year-old Westerner green with envy. Their lifestyle is living proof that maybe – just maybe – we're doing this whole 'progress' thing all wrong.

'We have two lives, and the second begins when we realise we only have one'.

Confucious

Because here in the West, progress often looks like more tech, more speed, more sitting, more stuff, more stress. We've forgotten simplicity and made room for convenience, and it's costing us. We strive for better, faster, stronger, but in the process, we've forgotten how to just *be*. The Tsimanes remind us that perhaps the way forward isn't the next big thing but instead, returning to what's always worked.

Now, let's be real, Tsimane life isn't all rainbows and perfect Insta moments. They face challenges, disease, infections and the encroachment of modern influences. Diabetes is beginning to rear its head as processed foods sneak into their world. But for now, they're still warriors, Martina included, resilient, strong and fiercely alive.

So here's the question: Are we chasing the wrong kind of progress? What if we took a leaf (or an entire tree) out of the Tsimane book? Less rush, more rhythm. Less stress, more connection. Less doing, more living. Less pessimism, more optimism. Maybe the future we're so desperate to create is waiting for us in the simplicity we've left behind.

The Tsimanes don't just defy time; they defy our excuses. The challenge is clear: if they can thrive deep in the jungle, what's stopping us from finding a little more vitality in our concrete ones?

Do Less Be More

So, what ties the Tsimanes and The Grand Plan of optimism together? It's fairly obvious, a simple truth we all know deep down: your mindset, your connections and the way you live your life are what make it worth living. That's it. Nothing fancy, no magic formulas. Just choices. Choices about who you spend your time with, how you treat others, and how you show up for yourself.

This book is ultimately about getting back to what matters, it's even in the subtitle! We all go through some shit at some point. Mental shit, physical shit, death shit, relationship shit, job shit, friend shit, big shit, scary shit, little shit, all-of-the-above-shit and *so* much other shit.

So, let's break it down.

The Grand Plan lays it out, optimism matters. It's not about skipping through the daisies with a big grin, it's about surrounding yourself with people who lift and fill you up. The kind who makes you feel bloody brilliant and remind you why life's worth the effort. And then there's the Tsimanes, deep in the Amazon, living the dream of connection. They're not just hanging about; they're thriving, together. Their community is a masterclass in how to live with heart.

The Grand Plan asks a tough question: what kind of friend are you? Are you the one people can count on, or are you the one always making excuses? It's not a comfy question, but it's an important one. And the Tsimanes? They're a mirror, showing us how life could be if we stripped away all the nonsense. They remind us to stop and ask, 'Am I living well, or just keeping up with the Joneses?'

I've learned anything worth having takes effort. The Grand Plan doesn't sugarcoat it; it's not easy to step away from toxic people or to put in the work for the ones who matter. And the Tsimanes? Their lives are built on effort. They don't have Netflix or Deliveroo, but what they do have is health, energy and a sense of purpose that puts most of us to shame.

Pessimism's a killer, plain and simple. The Grand Plan tells you to ditch it, and rightly so. It's dragging you down. Meanwhile, the Tsimanes show us what vitality looks like. Even when life throws them challenges, they meet them head-on and keep going. Resilience, optimism and strength, that's their secret.

The Takeaway?

Again, it's simple, really. I'll ask you for the second time in this chapter, what the bloody hell are you gonna do with this one wild, magical, terrifying, unpredictable, beautiful, tragically short wee life of yours? Are you living it, or are you just muddling through, making excuses? What do you want? The Grand Plan and the Tsimanes are two sides of the same coin, reminders that you've got the power to change things.

It's not about perfection. It's about trying. About choosing optimism over gloom, connection over loneliness and effort over apathy. It's about living a life that, when you look back, makes you smile and say, 'Aye, that was a gallus one'.

The Gospel of Gallus

Ah, *gallus*. My all-time favourite word. It rolls off the tongue like a cheeky wink from your granny after scalding you for nicking a penguin. The biscuit, not an actual penguin! *Gallus* is one of those magical Scottish inventions, a perfect cocktail of swagger, cheek and charm.

Gallus isn't just a word; it's a state of mind, a way of life even. It's the antidote to beige, the nemesis of boring and the ultimate badge of boldness. And who better to teach us about being gallus than the original feathered sass-master himself, the rooster.

The rooster, Gav? Really?

Yeah, this isn't as random as you might think . . .

Originally, thousands of years ago, the *Gallus Gallus Domesticus* was a type of chicken. But – spoiler alert – there's nothing chicken about being gallus. Then, around 1772, the term 'rooster' came into play, but the *Gallus Gallus* name stuck. Roosters are gallus. In fact, they're double gallus, literally!

Now, let me be clear, the rooster isn't just a cocky bird strutting about for the sake of it. Nope, this is a life coach in feathers, feathers so dazzling they'd make Elton John's wardrobe look like Primark!

When I say 'Life Coach', I do of course mean actual life coaches, qualified, not the pretend ones on Instagram. You know the ones. They're clearly just bored, have nothing to do and really really want to be famous so decide to pretend on Instagram that they're qualified to help you 'with your vibrations'. And then post pretty much nothing but selfies! FFS.

'Fold you worries into paper planes and turn them into flying fucks'.

Unknown

Back to roosters, obvs!

First off, the Rooster is the ultimate protector. They don't just puff up their chest for show. They'll fight tooth and claw to keep their flock safe, even if it means staring down a fox. That's gallus in action: standing tall and fearless in the face of danger, looking after your own and sounding the alarm when troubles afoot.

And if you think being gallus is all about shouting your head off, think again. Roosters are the ultimate timekeepers. Their crow is like a wake-up call to the world, and they don't do it just because they can, it's about purpose. They literally crow to let the world know; 'everything is ok'. It's part of the job, a reminder to find the good in every morning, starting each day with optimism. And sharing it. Being gallus is about owning your moment, knowing your worth, and reminding everyone else that they've got a place in the sun, too. (Man, I love that TV show so much.)

Roosters are also peacekeepers. Yup, those fiery feathers aren't just for show. They keep the others in line, break up squabbles, and make sure everyone gets a turn in the dust bath. Gallus isn't about being loud or overbearing, it's about balance. It's knowing when to intervene and when to just let things settle.

And let's not forget the strut. Have you ever seen a rooster walk? He's not just wandering about. It's a masterclass in confidence, head high, chest out, feathers gleaming like disco ball sequins. But he's not strutting because he's better than anyone else. He's strutting because he's *himself*. There's a difference. And that's gallus.

This book is for you, me, him, her, they and them. Channel your inner rooster today, flaunt what makes you different, what makes you you and let the world see *you* glimmer.

The Soft Serve Rebellion

So what was the glimmer in the back garden, Gav?

Weeks had passed since my life was flipped upside down. My year had been ruined, not even 10 nights in sunny Lanzarote could help.

I was pacing in the back garden, heavy-headed and exhausted from zero sleep, wondering (panicking) if I'd ever feel ok again when, out of nowhere, I heard it.

A tune.

Not just any tune. A jingle.

An unmistakable jingle at that.

This, this was the ice cream van jingle.

Now, I don't know about you, but I haven't seen an ice cream van on my street for years. It's one of those things that feels like it belongs in a different life, or at least in a summer that's long gone. But there it was. And for a second, I thought I might've imagined it. But nope, there it was again.

It wasn't just the music. It was the feeling it brought with it. The sunkick of all sunkicks. Suddenly, I was back in the days when I didn't worry about anything at all, just a kid running down the street, in Troon, on the west coast of Scotland, chasing the van with 50 pence in my hand and a whole world ahead of me.

It wasn't earth-shattering, but it was . . . nice.

It took me back to a time when things were simpler. Some might call it the Goonies era, when summer meant 99's, Mr Whippy, 2 Ball Screwballs, Fabs, Zooms, Mivvis, Troon beach, BMXs, Choppers, fronties, backies, Kwenchy Kups, hide 'n' seek, space hoppers, dens, the smell of childhood summers, picnics, sunburn, my brother, my parents, my childhood home. Me.

'Sometimes you never know the true value of a moment until it becomes a memory'.

Unknown

All from the ice cream van tune. A glimmer. Followed by a *much*-needed sunkick. A little reminder that joy doesn't always need to be complicated or deep. It just is, sometimes.

I'm not suggesting the ice cream van solved my problems, far from it. But in that moment, it was enough. It cut through the noise in my head, and for about 30 seconds I wasn't thinking about how I was feeling. It was a tiny glimmer of something good, breaking through the monotony.

The 'what ifs' were momentarily gone.

Think about *your* last unexpected moment of joy. What did it teach you? In a weird way, the ice cream van music was like a little reminder that not everything's as heavy as it feels. It was in this moment I knew I had to find more. I had to notice. I had to shift my thinking. Glimmers would light the way. I needed to be open to them. They would light me back up. They would fill me back up.

Everything Changes in the End

The more effort I put into my glimmer journey, the less stressed I am becoming and the easier I find it is to breathe. I've noticed less bothers me now. Dare I even say I'm more mindful . . .

Comedian Des Bishop makes the wonderful point that when we were kids no one mentioned the word 'mindfulness'. We were mindful 'half the fucking day'. We didn't have a choice. We didn't have phones in our pockets. He rightly points out that when we waited for someone, we waited . . . mindfulness. When you're on the bus, you were on the bus . . . mindfulness. Watching a condensation drip . . . mindfulness. When you rewound a VHS . . . mindfulness. He accurately observes that we used to take a shit . . . literally just shit . . . mindfulness!

He's right!

My mind feels more settled than before. When I fly, I no longer spend the journey with every ounce of my being tensed up as I try to keep the plane in the sky with my mind. Stuck in traffic? Love it. Housework? Whatevs. IKEA? Easy. One of the biggest shifts for me is the fact I no longer wake up with my first thought being, 'What do I need to worry about today?'

'I have found that if you love life, life will love you back'.

Arthur Rubinstein

Life is not for overthinking. Yes, we're bloody complicated (and amazing), but never forget, despite all our accomplishments as humans, we owe our entire existence to a six-inch layer of topsoil and the fact it rains. That's it, there is no need to fill your life with unrequired pressure, do you think nature worries about what to post on LinkedIn or which way the toilet roll faces?

And next time you wonder if you matter or wonder if you're making a difference in the world, just remember, somewhere, out there, someone carries a piece of you with them. Maybe it's the way you stood up when life tried to kick your ass, or how you made them smile when everything else felt like it was burning. Maybe it's your unshakable belief that things can be better. Maybe it's just the way you dare to give a shit. Maybe it's your kindness.

They saw you. They felt it. And something in them shifted.

You may never know who, or when, or how. But trust me, you have been someone's turning point. Their moment of clarity. Their quiet reason to keep going. Their glimmer *and* their sunkick!

Because when you showed up, flawed and real and raw, you gave permission for others to do the same. You didn't have to be perfect to make an impact, it was never about that. It was the messy, wonderful, ridiculous humanness of you that made the difference.

You have left ripples in places you've never been, and you know nothing about it. Your presence has softened hearts, sparked rebellion, lit fires and ignited laughter. You maybe even saved someone without ever knowing it.

So, if you ever wonder whether you matter, let me tell you: You do. You always have and you always will.

Congrats, You're Alive . . .

My main goal in life now? Just to have a good day.

Weekend plans? Have a good day.

Five-year plan? Same. Have a good day.

Why? Because *these* are the good old days.

Everything you're doing right now, your 90-year-old self would trade anything to come back and feel it all again. This is it. This is your life. Let it sunkick the hell out of you.

Glass half empty? Glass half full? Honestly, who cares?

The real question is, do I even have a glass?

Cool. That's a start.

A full heart and a fed mind matter more anyway, so let's just be grateful for the damn glass.

Also, you might not know this, but off-days are allowed.

Sometimes the most powerful thing you can be is *completely unimpressive.*

Not every day needs to be legendary. You don't always have to perfect, hustle (awful word) or achieve.

Some days, just being a potato on the couch is enough. And guess what?

Potato days matter.

And when things seem especially rough just ask yourself, 'Did I shit my pants today?' And if the answer is no, you're doing alright.

The glimmers. Always the glimmers.

Keep in mind, no one gets out alive. Everything changes in the end. We have one go. One shot. And then we die.

And when I die, I give you all permission to use my death for personal gain. Even if you don't know me, you go and tell your boss that a good friend has died and take a day just for you. Sleep in. Do nothing. Eat a box of ice-lollies. That ones on me.

Until then, all I ask in return is this: believe that you matter. Know that you are loved. Accept the world is better for having you in it, and you never *ever* let anyone tell you you're not magic.

Just remember, making the world a better place for *all* matters too, because life isn't beautiful until it's beautiful for everyone.

Til death do us party . . .

'Before you diagnose yourself with depression or low self-esteem, first make sure that you are not, in fact, just surrounded by assholes'.

Anon

Acknowledgements

I've got nothing clever to say here, just the truth. This book exists because something shit happened, and I broke. Instead of sweeping it under the rug, I wrote my way through it.

Ali, you know. You were there. It might be my name on the front but you're in every page. I love you, thank you. Cups of tea forever.

To my kids, actual magic in human form. Thank you for being the daily reminder that joy doesn't need permission.

Team TOK, you never even flinched. Thank you.

To my publisher, thank you for not asking me to tidy this up and for letting me write like I feel. Nick and Annie, you've always had my back, thank you.

Pete, you got it immediately and made this thing look beautiful. Thank you.

My therapist, Alison. Thank you for helping me unpick the knots without letting me come undone.

And to you – whoever you are, wherever you are – if you've found a little piece of yourself inside these pages, believe me, there are loads of us.

No glory, no glittering finale.

Just this: thank you.

And a reminder: you made it here too. Don't you dare forget that.

About the Author

Gavin Oattes is not your average keynote speaker or writer; he is an experiment of one. An award-winning comedian, bestselling author and one of the most inspirational voices on the planet today.

With a unique cocktail of razor-sharp wit, heartfelt storytelling and boundless enthusiasm, Gavin doesn't just talk *at* his audience, he takes them on a high-energy, laugh-out-loud, soul-stirring journey. Whether he's opening an international conference, wrapping up a leadership summit or writing his books, Gavin's mission is simple: to remind people of their brilliance, their resilience and that magical spark they've been carrying around since childhood.

Sought after by the world's leading brands, Gavin speaks on themes that matter – *wellbeing, leadership, playfulness, engagement, resilience* – with a style that blends hilarity with humanity. He doesn't deal in jargon or fluff. He deals in moments. The kind that sticks with you long after the applause dies down.

Millions have been moved by his words. Even more have rediscovered their 'wee piece of magic' because of them.

Gavin is a man who believes in the wonder of people, the power of kindness and the unshakeable truth that a good laugh and a wee bit of hope can change everything.

ALSO AVAILABLE BY
GAVIN OATTES

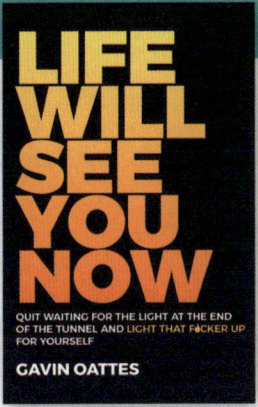

9780857088086
Life Will See You Now

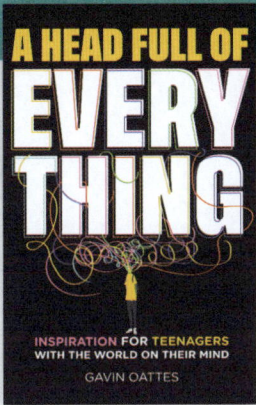

9780857089014
A Head Full of Everything

9780857087652
Shine

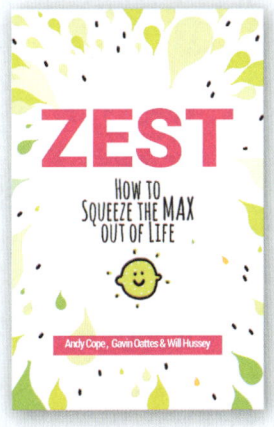

9780857088000
Zest

9780857087867
Diary of a Brilliant Kid

9780857088918
Brill Kid - The Big Number 2

AVAILABLE WHEREVER
BOOKS ARE SOLD